D0555313

Smarty

PHP Template Programming and Applications

A step-by-step guide to building PHP web sites and applications using the Smarty templating engine

João Prado Maia
Hasin Hayder
Lucian Gheorghe

BIRMINGHAM - MUMBAI

Smarty

PHP Template Programming and Applications

First published: April 2006

Production Reference: 1050406

Published by Packt Publishing Ltd.
32 Lincoln Road
Olton
Birmingham, B27 6PA, UK.

ISBN 1-904811-40-X

www.packtpub.com

Cover Design by www.visionwt.com

Credits

Authors
João Prado Maia
Hasin Hayder
Lucian Gheorghe

Reviewer
Mizanur Rahman

Technical Editor
Rushabh Sanghavi

Editorial Manager
Dipali Chittar

Development Editor
David Barnes

Indexer
Ashutosh Pande

Proofreader
Chris Smith

Production Coordinator
Manjiri Nadkarni

Cover Designer
Helen Wood

About the Authors

João Prado Maia is Lead Software Developer with Alert Logic, Inc. and was previously with MySQL AB as the lead developer behind Eventum, an issue tracking system, and MySQL Network, a subscription product for everything related to MySQL services. He has been working with PHP, Smarty, and PEAR for several years, and maintains phpbrasil.com, one of the most popular PHP-related community sites in Brazil. He is also interested in fostering a community of PHP developers in Houston by organizing the Houston PHP Users Group at `http://houstonphp.org`.

I would like to thank my wife for her encouragement and patience while I was writing chapters for this book. I dedicate my work to you, Juliana.

Hasin Hayder graduated in Civil Engineering from Rajshahi University of Engineering and Technology (RUET). He is an open-source enthusiast who has been programming since early 2001. He maintains phpXperts, the largest PHP user group in Bangladesh, and Zephyr, an open-source AJAX-based MVC framework for PHP5 developers. He is currently working as a web application developer in a Norwegian software development company, "Somewhere In...". You can reach him at `hasin@somewherein.net`.

I would like to thank my editors from Packt Publishing, David Barnes, Rushabh Sanghavi, and Patricia Weir for this book. Without them I doubt I would have completed my chapters so easily. I would also like to thank Damian and Arnab in Packt Publishing for their help.

Thanks also go to Mom, Dad, all my family members, Mahbub bhai, Rashidul Hasan and all my friends for supporting me. And finally I would like to thank Ashikuzzaman Fahim and Arild Klokkerhaug, who inspire me a lot.

I would like to dedicate this book to my wife and my best friend Ayesha. I know I could not live here without you.

Lucian Gheorghe is currently working as a senior network engineer for Globtel Internet, a significant Internet and Telephony Services Provider to the Romanian market. Even if it's not his main activity, He has been programming in PHP for over 5 years building billing interfaces, industrial software interfaces, e-commerce sites, and so on. He had a lot of help from a friend called Smarty in his programming experiences.

Lucian got his first taste of writing when he contributed a few chapters to the book *Beginning PHP 5 and MySQL E-Commerce* by Cristian Darie and Mihai Bucica, Apress, 2004, with his appendix for Project Management added to the book *Beginning ASP.NET 2.0 E-Commerce in C# 2005* by Cristian Darie and Karli Watson, Apress, 2005.

I would like to thank you for buying this book, my parents for everything they did for me, my girlfriend who stood by me, the team at Globtel, which is like a second family for me and last, but not least a very good friend, the greatest technical author alive—Cristian Darie.

About the Reviewer

Mizanur Rahman is a Computer Science graduate from North South University, Bangladesh. He has 7 years of programming experience and vast knowledge on open-source technologies. He has more than 5 years of experience on working with PHP and PHP-related tools and technologies. Currently he is working as a full time senior software engineer in a USA-based software company located in Dhaka.

Table of Contents

Smarty for Designers

Smarty for Programmers

Preface

Smarty is a powerful templating tool that can breathe new life into PHP programming, and solve many of the difficulties PHP programmers face on non-trivial projects.

This book will take you through the Smarty basics step by step, showing you how to realize the benefits from this product. But this is no "hello world" tutorial; the book also covers advanced Smarty topics crucial to large-scale web development: performance, internationalization, customization, and so on.

Smarty is an established engine with a proven track record for making development and design easier and more elegant. Whether you're just starting with Smarty, or are looking for extra insights on advanced features, this book will help you.

What This Book Covers

The first two chapters are an introduction to Smarty. The remaining chapters of the book are divided into two main sections. Chapters 3-7 deal with Smarty template design, and are aimed primarily at designers. The later chapters get more technical, showing how programmers can work with Smarty and PHP to create complex, interactive and high performance applications. Here's what each chapter covers:

Chapter 1 will ease you into the world of Smarty. Starting with an overview of what templating systems are and why you use them, it goes on to consider Smarty specifically. Once that's covered, you'll see how to install Smarty so you're ready to begin your Smarty development.

Chapter 2 discusses how Smarty can make projects easier for programmers and designers, reduce the time taken on programming and maintenance, and bring harmony to the fraught relationship between designers and programmers. You'll then see how to start your first n-tier Smarty project.

Chapter 3 is a designer's overview of Smarty, explaining the key concepts and how designers can create versatile and attractive templates and layouts.

Chapter 4 looks at templates in detail, showing how values pass into templates and how to use them in applications such as calendars, database-backed reports, email newsletters and more.

Chapter 5 covers more advanced ways to work with templates, including how to play with variables right in the template using modifiers.

Chapter 6 delves into the programming side of Smarty. There are many powerful functions that designers can use to make Smarty development easier and more productive. This chapter introduces the most useful of these, and provides practical examples of functions in action.

With all the added power in the designer's hands, there are bound to be mistakes occasionally.

Chapter 7 will introduce you to methods for debugging your Smarty templates, so that you'll be able to find why the wrong values are being displayed, or that pesky extra <td> tag is ruining your layout.

Chapter 8 starts with more technical aspects of Smarty. You will see how built-in variables and methods bring added functionality to your PHP code, with very little extra work.

Chapter 9 looks at how Smarty can make the code itself faster. This in-depth look at Smarty's caching and performance features, and how to optimize your code for them, will enable you to write very scalable and fast applications with Smarty.

Chapter 10 pushes Smarty even further, showing how to extend its capabilities with downloadable plug-ins, and even showing how to write your own.

Chapter 11 takes a detailed look at filters, which are a special kind of plug-in.

Chapter 12 concludes the book with a look at how to make your website available in different locales and languages using Smarty's internationalization features.

Conventions

In this book, you will find a number of styles of text that distinguish between different kinds of information. Here are some examples of these styles, and an explanation of their meaning.

There are three styles for code. Code words in text are shown as follows: "We can include other contexts through the use of the `include` directive."

A block of code will be set as follows:

```php
<?php
include_once('libs/Smarty.class.php');
$smarty = new Smarty;
$smarty->caching = 1;
$smarty->display('example2.tpl');
?>
```

When we wish to draw your attention to a particular part of a code block, the relevant lines or items will be made bold:

```php
<?php
include_once('libs/Smarty.class.php');
$smarty = new Smarty;
$smarty->caching = 1;
$smarty->display('example2.tpl');
?>
```

Any command-line input and output is written as follows:

$ xgettext -o smartybook.po -n *.php

New terms and **important words** are introduced in a bold-type font. Words that you see on the screen, in menus or dialog boxes for example, appear in our text like this: "clicking the Next button moves you to the next screen".

Warnings or important notes appear in a box like this.

Tips and tricks appear like this.

Reader Feedback

Feedback from our readers is always welcome. Let us know what you think about this book, what you liked or may have disliked. Reader feedback is important for us to develop titles that you really get the most out of.

To send us general feedback, simply drop an email to feedback@packtpub.com, making sure to mention the book title in the subject of your message.

If there is a book that you need and would like to see us publish, please send us a note in the SUGGEST A TITLE form on www.packtpub.com or email suggest@packtpub.com.

If there is a topic that you have expertise in and you are interested in either writing or contributing to a book, see our author guide on www.packtpub.com/authors.

Customer Support

Now that you are the proud owner of a Packt book, we have a number of things to help you to get the most from your purchase.

Downloading the Example Code for the Book

Visit http://www.packtpub.com/support, and select this book from the list of titles to download any example code or extra resources for this book. The files available for download will then be displayed.

The downloadable files contain instructions on how to use them.

Errata

Although we have taken every care to ensure the accuracy of our contents, mistakes do happen. If you find a mistake in one of our books—maybe a mistake in text or code—we would be grateful if you would report this to us. By doing this you can save other readers from frustration, and help to improve subsequent versions of this book. If you find any errata, report them by visiting http://www.packtpub.com/support, selecting your book, clicking on the Submit Errata link, and entering the details of your errata. Once your errata have been verified, your submission will be accepted and the errata added to the list of existing errata. The existing errata can be viewed by selecting your title from http://www.packtpub.com/support.

Questions

You can contact us at questions@packtpub.com if you are having a problem with some aspect of the book, and we will do our best to address it.

1
Introduction to Smarty

Today, websites are past the level of presenting summary and contact data for companies and projects. With the evolution of the Internet, most websites are now stand-alone businesses rather than summary presentations of companies. More than that, complex applications' developers have embraced the idea of using websites as interfaces for their software.

For more than ten years, PHP has been one of the best choices for web developers being the most complete open-source web programming language. With growth of the complexity of PHP applications, a new problem that was raised was, *how to separate programmers' code (PHP) from designers' code (HTML)*, or better phrased, *how to separate the content from presentation*.

Smarty, a PHP templating system, was born to solve this problem.

Templating Systems

The basic functionality of a templating system is introducing a way of separating presentation from content with very little interaction between programmers and designers. For example, the design of a website may look like this:

Header	
Nav	Content
Footer	

The designers build the *face* of the website with pictures, text styles, tables, and so on. They build *templates* for how to arrange the content in each page.

The only information the designers need is how the site should look and whether they need to layout content like news, products, jokes, and so on.

On the other hand, programmers code the application using PHP to do data manipulation (business logic). They are not interested in how the website looks (colors, pictures, text styles) or where the content is laid out on the page. All they need to do is pass the content to the templates using variable names they agree upon with the designers.

This is roughly how template systems work. Starting from this basic functionality, every template system has a set of features that makes it easier for both designers and programmers if they are well documented in the template system they use.

This book is intended to show you how to use all the features offered by Smarty in the optimum way.

Why Use a Templating System?

Building a website is similar to creating software. It can be done by building it from scratch, just starting to write code to see what you can come up with at the end and solving problems on the way; or it can be done by differentiating the project's components into separate layers and building the website taking these layers into consideration. This is called multi-tier or multi-level software architecture. If the website is a small one containing only a few lines of PHP code, the first option might work. Just create a few tables in a database, start coding with PHP, maybe create a few banners, generate a few tables and debug every step. People like it this way—fast and easy.

When it comes to more complicated web-based projects such as web portals, e-commerce sites, ERP systems, and so on, the first option may work but in most cases it can very difficult to achieve anything by coding away. Besides, with the market being so crowded with web projects, in order for your website to stand a chance, you have to have a great layout which is appropriate for the type of project you are building and of course, stable code tested in all situations. That's why people involved in building websites specialize either in designing great layouts (web designers), or in programming very well (web programmers). Not often will you see a good web programmer creating great designs, or a good web designer writing good, bug-free code.

A software company that creates websites usually has a design department and a programming department, and most medium to large web projects always have a programmer as well as a designer working on them.

Programmers have different ways of coding applications and if they use only PHP without a template engine, the designer will need to be familiar with every programmer's way of arranging the code, naming variables, and so on. Also, the programmer will need to understand the designer's templates and generate the code to print HTML code from PHP where the designer wants it.

Let's take the following example:

```
for ( $col = 1; $col < $i; $col++ ) {
    print "<tr> <td> $procesid[$col]</td> <td>$data[$col] </td>
<td>$value[$col]</td> </tr>"; }
```

This is PHP code that prints the values of three arrays in a table. Even a simple example like this one is hard to read and to arrange in a web page exactly as desired.

With Smarty, the PHP syntax doesn't contain *print*. Instead, the programmer passes these arrays to the designer by assigning them to Smarty templates. Then it's the designer's job to make them look good in the web page without worrying about the PHP code. This is one big benefit about using Smarty, and we will learn in this book how this is done.

The Smartness of Smarty

Smarty allows designers and programmers to interoperate more effectively and not worry about each other's work. The designer builds the templates for the web page layout and extracts the data from the PHP files that the programmer has created. The programmer passes data to the templates without having to generate HTML code. This way, everyone is happy and more efficient because they all do the job they are good at.

Let's think about an e-commerce site that sells laptop computers. The manufacturer's name, the model number, characteristics, and price are content elements that will be stored in a database and displayed to the visitor.

Smarty makes the job of the designer as well as the programmer very easy. The key tasks performed by them can be listed as follows.

The Programmer's tasks:

- Extract database elements with a simple query on the database.
- Validate and manipulate the data by performing business logic on it.
- If needed, change the data access methods and the business logic without interfering with the designer's work. For example, the whole system could migrate from MySQL to PostgreSQL without the designer making a single change.

The Designer's tasks:

- Create HTML designs without affecting or jeopardizing the programmers PHP code. The designer only needs to be concerned with placing the content elements that the programmer has agreed to provide.
- Make changes to the design without consulting or interfering with the programmer's work.
- Stop worrying about technical changes to the site breaking the way that the site appears to viewers.

In the above example, we see that tasks are assigned to people involved in the project depending on the parts they are working on—presentation, business, and data access.

Later in this chapter we'll have a look at the process of building software applications, including websites, using multi-tier architecture.

Smarty Alternatives

For most people who need a PHP templating system, Smarty is the natural choice mainly because of its popularity. As you probably know, Smarty is not the only PHP template engine in the market, but it is the most complete and reliable one.

From the variety of other PHP template engines, we would mention the following:

- PHP Savant: `http://phpsavant.com/yawiki/`
- PHPlib: `http://phplib.sourceforge.net/`
- Yats: `http://yats.sourceforge.net/`
- FastTemplate: `http://www.thewebmasters.net/php/FastTemplate.pHTML`
- SimpleTemplate: `http://simplet.sourceforge.net/`
- Yapter: `http://yapter.sourceforge.net/`
- patTemplate: `http://www.php-tools.de/site.php?file=/patTemplate/overview.xml`

Most of these PHP templating systems have a few advantages like speed and ease of use, mainly because they are not as complex as Smarty. However Smarty has more features than most of its competitors and it can be customized to be pretty fast.

In my opinion, the true competitor of Smarty is PHP Savant, which is a powerful but lightweight object-oriented template system for PHP. Savant includes a lot of Smarty's features.

However, there is one big difference between Smarty and Savant that can be either an advantage or a big disadvantage for Savant, depending on which point of view you are looking at. The difference is that templates in Savant are written in PHP and not in another language like Smarty introduces. This can be:

- An advantage for Savant—Designers work with PHP as a template language, they don't have to learn another templating language.
- A disadvantage for Savant and a huge advantage for Smarty concerning security. Savant doesn't compile the templates into PHP as the templates themselves are PHP files. This way, designers have access to the full power of PHP. If the designer is not a trusted one Savant is out of the question and Smarty is the answer.

In most cases, designers are not trusted to have access to the systems where web pages run, therefore Smarty is still the best templating system for PHP. Savant is nice, but it almost totally lacks security, while other template engines have only some parts of the functionality Smarty has.

A Rough Guide to the Software Design Process

The process of building a website involves a few steps that may vary from project to project, but generally it is the same for most projects.

The first step is to establish the customer needs, on which you design a database. These needs are later transcribed in a spoken agreement or preferably in a document. This document should contain a description of the desired functionality of the software as well as the definition of the database tables with explanations for every column. Once the customer agrees on this document and maybe makes a few changes, you can start the actual process of building the website.

If you are your own customer this is not the case, otherwise it is my strong opinion that you should do this. For one of my first projects, I skipped the document part and it led to a total fiasco. The customer wanted more and more and did not want to pay more for it, but if the document had existed he would have had no choice.

The next step is to create and show a few layouts to the customer. This is the designer's job. He or she will work with the customer and come up with a design that the customer likes. After the customer finalizes a design, the actual building of the website begins. When the project is finished, the customer has a testing period in which a few modifications are made or some bugs cleared, and it's done.

This is beautiful in theory, but in real life, programmers speak languages like PHP and SQL and designers speak in HTML and CSS, and they often tend to have a few differences.

Working in Teams: Layers and Separation of Concerns

When human interactions might fail, it's preferable to separate the work as much as possible. Multi-tier software architecture should do the job. The most commonly used architecture is one with three tiers or layers. These are:

- Presentation Logic Layer
- Business Logic Layer
- Data Access Layer

Separating these layers in project development cycles allows you to achieve rapid application development with project maintainability in mind.

In the three-tier architecture, the interaction between layers is shown in the following diagram:

Starting from the bottom, at the **Data Access Layer** we find both the data and the ways to extract the data that we want to show to the user. The Data Access Layer may contain:

- A database (MySQL, PostgreSQL, MSSQL, and so on) and the SQL language used to extract data from the database
- Files that store data and PHP functions (or other languages) that parse the files
- Data acquisition software (for example, a thermometer on the parallel port)

Now that we've extracted the data, we need to manipulate it in order to get the results we need to display. Data manipulation and validation is done at the **Business Logic Layer**, which may contain:

- Data validation based on the business plan (for example, list only in-stock items)
- Data manipulation according to the business plan (for example, discounts, stock liquidations, and so on)
- Functions and formulas to calculate things like shipping expenses, and so on.

The **Presentation Logic Layer** is where the web page layout—how data from the Business Logic Layer is arranged in the web page—is defined. This is done using:

- Web page templates
- Text/CSS styles
- Images, banners, and menu styles

Without a templating engine at the Presentation Logic Layer, we find HTML and PHP creating the layout with pure HTML and generating HTML code from PHP. In this case, we cannot divide the Presentation Logic and Business Logic layers into two separate layers, making the work of designers and programmers very difficult for complex software projects. That's where Smarty comes in.

Smarty—The Ultimate Templating System for PHP

Now that we've decided to make our life easier by considering multi-tier architecture for our website, we should take a look at what Smarty can do, as well as what it can't do for us.

Smarty is not built for separating HTML from PHP; instead, its primary goal is to separate the application logic from presentation logic. If Smarty's goal was to separate PHP from HTML then the presentation layer would contain no logic; but Smarty templates can contain logic, as long as it is to be used for presentation only.

This may seem like it breaks the rules of rigid separation between layers and tasks, but there are good practical reasons for it. A simple example would be an e-commerce site with products displayed in four columns:

- **Without Smarty**: If our presentation layer doesn't contain logic, we need to modify the business logic to retrieve the products in four arrays.
- **With Smarty**: Using logic in the templates, the programmer just passes the products to the templates in a single array and the designer arranges the products in the page as he or she desires.

Smarty offers an interface to pretty much all of PHP, so PHP can be included in the templates, but it's recommended to leave most of PHP code at the business logic layer. Fortunately, Smarty's logic is generally much simpler to use than PHP and designers do not need to become programmers in order to incorporate presentation logic into their Smarty designs.

Is Smarty Fast?

Template systems introduce another level of processing in the application, so we might suspect that Smarty applications will run slower than plain PHP equivalents. Basically, we have a new pseudo-scripting language (the template engine's tags) inside our scripting language (PHP).

Smarty is extremely fast by doing what is called *template compiling*. That means that it reads the templates, creates PHP scripts from them and includes the PHP files, resulting in a single PHP script that is compiled by the PHP engine, which is pretty fast. The beauty of the process is that the templates are parsed only once by Smarty, and only templates that are modified are *compiled* again. This is done automatically by Smarty and results in a fast compilation done by the PHP engine with very little overhead from Smarty.

If you are concerned about the performance of your site, Smarty has built-in caching support that can speed things up, especially on websites that have content that is not modified very often. You can cache all the content of a web page or only some of it and you can specify for how long Smarty should keep the content cached. This will be explained in more detail in Chapter 9.

Since Smarty does *template compiling* resulting in a PHP script, there is no reason why we should not use a PHP compiler cache solution like PHP Accelerator or Zend Cache.

PHP Accelerator and Zend Cache have no problem with Smarty's output and cache the PHP scripts produced by Smarty very well, so if our main concern is performance we should use one of these caching solutions combined with Smarty's built-in caching support.

Is Smarty Secure?

We concluded that Smarty is fast, but we need to know about its security, which according to me is most important for any website.

By default, when using Smarty you are theoretically as secure as you are when using only PHP. This means that by using Smarty you can't be less secure than using PHP only; but Smarty has some features to improve security in case this is needed.

When a site is built by a programmer working with a designer without using Smarty, the designer has access to the application and can modify all the PHP scripts. This is not good for security because a designer with bad intentions can breach the security of the system very easily when he or she has all the power of PHP in his or her hands.

Smarty comes with some built-in security features for situations where unreliable parties edit templates. When security is set on templates, a designer who modifies templates via an unsecured connection like FTP is unlikely to gain access in the system.

Using Smarty security features, you can:

- Allow or deny usage of PHP code in the templates
- Allow only a set of PHP functions as variable modifiers
- Restrict the folders from which templates can be included
- Restrict the folders from which local files can be fetched by templates

My strong advice is to always think about security. Think about having a database with credit card details and your designer including unsafe PHP code in one web page. This would result in a disaster for your business.

Smarty's Main Features

Smarty offers both designers and programmers tools to optimize their work. Reading this entire book you will find out about all these wonderful features and will see how great Smarty is. Let's preview some of these features and look at the reasons why they should or should not be used.

Variable Modifiers

When displaying content on a website, you might want to change some of it depending on the time or visitor's origin. For example, we might want to show a date in different formats. Using Smarty, there's no need for the programmer's intervention for this. He or she will just pass the date in the proper variable to the template, and the designer can format the date however he or she desires.

Also, the designer can upper-case or lower-case a variable, truncate a text block, add spaces between characters, and so on and it's all done at display-time with Smarty.

Think about displaying a product category as a small title in uppercase and with spaces between the word's characters (for example, 'C A R S'). In the database, the corresponding column contains the word 'cars'. With Smarty you don't have to ask the programmer to change it to 'C A R S'. When he or she passes the variable to the template, you can do that with proper variable modifiers at display-time, and again, if you want to modify the way you display the product category later (for example, 'Cars'), this doesn't require the programmer's intervention.

You will learn more about variable modifiers in Chapter 5.

Template Functions

While going through Smarty's syntax you will discover another great thing about Smarty— Template Functions. Think about designing a large form with many HTML dropdowns. The old-fashioned way to do this is to write tags for every drop-down menu. With Smarty, you can simply write a function for dropdowns and call it every time you need to display one, making things simpler and faster. This was an easy example, but you can save a lot of time writing functions for displaying content in manners that you repeat frequently.

You will learn more about template functions in Chapter 6.

Debugging

At every step of building a software application, programmers and designers need debugging to easily correct their work.

Think how much time you can lose if you misspell a variable and don't have debugging tools. In my experience as a programmer, that's the worst scenario, even worse than having mistakes in your algorithm.

Even if you can debug with PHP, Smarty provides a debugging console for correcting Smarty-related errors. This is a very powerful debugging tool, as you are informed of all the included templates, assigned variables and configuration file variables for the current template.

With Smarty you can modify the format of the debugging console, so you can highlight the things you find important in debugging. In addition, you can dump the output of the debugging console to the page using a Smarty function in the template, but since Smarty's functions are executed at run time, you can only see the variables involved not the templates included.

You will learn more about debugging with Smarty in Chapter 7.

Plug-ins

One very important thing for a business that develops software is the possibility to reuse code. This saves time and money when new projects are built that contain functionality related to other projects created before, and this is what really makes a software business profitable. Using code from one application in another with copy and paste requires modification of variables, function names, retesting and careful integration with the new application, but is faster rather than rewriting the piece of code.

However, there is a better method for reusing code—using **Plug-ins**. When building a site, identify functionalities that can be reused even in the same project and create them as plug-ins. This way, after building a few sites, you will have a portfolio of plug-ins that run well and can be included without modifications in any new project saving a lot of time and work. For doing this, we need to have plug-in support in the software that we use to build our project.

Smarty has a plug-in architecture that is used for most of its customizable functionality. With Smarty, you can write plug-ins for functions, compiler functions, block functions, modifiers, resources, inserts, prefilters, postfilters, and output filters.

A lot of software out there with plug-in architecture loads all plug-ins before compiling. This is not necessarily wrong, but Smarty's designers kept performance in mind and made the plug-ins load only when they are invoked in a template. More than that, a plug-in invoked once in a template is only loaded once, even if there are more instances of Smarty requesting the same plug-in.

For example, when creating an e-commerce site, you can create plug-ins for the shopping basket functionality or filters for currency conversion that you can use later in other e-commerce projects you build, without having to write the same code again but being paid similar amounts of money.

You will learn more about plug-ins in Chapter 10.

Filters

Disciplined designers may write a lot of comments in their templates, resulting in a big file after compilation. Smarty's developers thought about this and included a set of filters to solve this problem. Smarty has **prefilters**, which are PHP functions that the templates are run through before they are compiled. With prefilters you can modify anything in the templates before *template compilation*. For example, if you want to remove all the comments you can do that very easily using a prefilter.

However, if you want to add some comments to the compiled templates you can do that with **postfilters**. Smarty's postfilters are PHP functions that the templates are run through after they are compiled.

You can also filter out the content of a template by using **output filters**, which are PHP functions used for filtering the output of a template when it is executed, for example replacing banned words with *, hiding email addresses, and so on. With these powerful filters, the programmer has complete control over the templates.

You will learn more about prefilters, postfilters, and output filters in Chapter 11.

Smarty Internals

From the designer's point of view, Smarty is a new simple and powerful scripting language that can be used together with HTML to simplify the work with the programmer. Also, the new scripting language that Smarty introduces to designers offers them ways to simplify their work.

A very eloquent example to my previous statement would be the following syntax:

```
<select name="Employee">
  {HTML_options options=$names}
</select>
```

The first and last lines are HTML but the line in the middle is Smarty. This line creates select options with values in the $names array that is received from the programmer. In this way, the designer only has to ask the programmer to pass employee names in an array named $names (minimum interaction). Instead of writing <option></option> a lot of times, the designer uses a Smarty function that simplifies his or her work.

Instead of placing the above example in an HTML file, the designer places it in a file with the .tpl extension and tells the programmer the full name of the template (.tpl) file.

This book has a section called *Smarty for Designers* in which designers will learn this new scripting language with useful examples, tips, and tricks from the authors' experience.

From the programmer's point of view, Smarty is a large PHP class with variables and methods. The name of the class is smarty, so to assign a Smarty class variable, the programmer must do:

```
$smarty = new Smarty;
```

The Smarty class offers programmers more efficient ways of interacting with designers. For example, say the designer requested all employee names in a variable named $names. After extracting the names from the database in an array, the programmer passes these to the designer. This can be done by simply adding:

```
$smarty->assign('names',$names_array);
```

For the programmer, one of the best things about Smarty is that there's no need to have HTML code in the PHP files. HTML code is in the `.tpl` files which are displayed using one of the Smarty class methods:

```
$smarty->display("index.tpl");
```

The second section of this book is called *Smarty for Programmers*. Reading this section, programmers will learn about the Smarty class and how to use it in the best way.

Installing and Configuring Smarty

Smarty is distributed under the **GNU Lesser General Public License**, which is the successor for the GNU Library General Public License. The difference between the Lesser GPL and the old Library GPL is that the software is less protected in the Lesser GPL, meaning that the libraries distributed under this license are free software and can be used to create commercial software. The old Library GPL allows you to use the software distributed under its license only to create free software.

The point is that Smarty is a free tool, and we can create commercial software using Smarty without paying for it.

If you want to make sure you are 100% legal, you can read the entire Lesser General Public License at `http://www.gnu.org/copyleft/lesser.html`.

Step 1: Obtaining Smarty

You can download the latest stable Smarty source code from Smarty's website at `http://smarty.php.net/download.php`. Always make sure to download the latest release as it contains bug fixes for all the previous versions.

Smarty is, in fact, a library for PHP and its requirements are very simple: a web server with PHP 4.0.6 or later. Apache can be used as a web server since it's the most popular choice, but it's not the only one. Instructions on installing Apache can be found at `http://www.apache.org`.

After downloading Smarty from the web server and uncompressing the archive, we have a folder with the current Smarty distribution. In the distribution root you will find a folder named `libs`, which contains the following files and folders:

- `smarty.class.php`
- `smarty_Compiler.class.php`
- `config_File.class.php`
- `debug.tpl`
- `\internals`
- `\plug-ins`

All these files are needed to run Smarty applications and the PHP files are not to be edited.

Step 2: Configure PHP to Find the Smarty Libraries

The simple method of installing Smarty is to add the libs folder path to the include path in the php.ini file.

On Windows

A very simple but effective way to configure Smarty would be to first create a folder, say mycode in the document root of your Apache installation. Next, copy the libs folder from the Smarty distribution to the mycode folder (for example, c:\apache\htdocs\mycode\libs\).

After this, you need to edit the php.ini file and add include_path = ".;c:\apache\htdocs\ mycode\libs\" where c:\apache\htdocs\mycode\libs\ represents the location of your libs folder.

On Linux

For example, let's say you've extracted the distribution of Smarty you downloaded in /usr/local/Smarty.

Just edit the php.ini file and add include_path = ".:/usr/local/Smarty/libs" and it's all set. You can also copy the libs folder to any location of the include_path in php.ini if you don't want to edit the file.

This is the easiest way to install Smarty. The point is that you need to load the smarty.class.php file in every PHP file that uses Smarty templates, so if you have it in one folder of the PHP include path, you can create a Smarty instance for it by:

```
<?php
require('Smarty.class.php');
$smarty = new Smarty;
?>
```

After setting everything up, you have to change the permission of your templates_c folder, which resides in your script path. That means your code and the templates_c folder must remain in the same directory. Now using FTP just change the permissions of your templates_c folder to 777 (rwxrwxrwx).

You can perform this action using the following shell command:

```
chmod -R 0777 templates_c
```

An Alternative to Step 2: Using Smarty without Having Full Access to the System

If you don't have access to modify the php.ini file or to copy Smarty libs in one of the folders of the php include_path, you can still use Smarty by setting the Smarty libs directory in the PHP files that use Smarty.

Smarty uses a PHP constant called SMARTY_DIR, which doesn't need to be set in the first case when you edit the php.ini file to include the Smarty libs. However, you can manually set the SMARTY_DIR to point to the same path as the Smarty libs.

- For Windows:

```php
<?php
define('SMARTY_DIR', 'C:\apache\htdocs\mycode\libs\);
require(SMARTY_DIR . 'Smarty.class.php');
$smarty = new Smarty;
?>
```

- For Linux:

```php
<?php
define('SMARTY_DIR', '/usr/local/Smarty/libs');
require(SMARTY_DIR . 'Smarty.class.php');
$smarty = new Smarty;
?>
```

> Note that since there are so many ways of using Smarty. In this book, we will assume that you copied the libs folder from Smarty's distribution root to the mycode folder within your Apache document root and added its location to the php.ini file. If you are using Linux, we also assume that you have changed the permissions of the templates_c folder to 777 or rwxrwxrwx.

Step 3: Set Up Smarty for Your Application

After we are sure that we can find the smarty.class.php file, we need to set up the folders for our application. Every Smarty application needs four folders, which are named by default templates, templates_c, configs, and cache.

Each of these folders can be defined by the Smarty class proprieties $template_dir, $compile_dir, $config_dir, and $cache_dir. Every Smarty application should have its own folders.

For Linux, Smarty needs write access to $compile_dir and $cache_dir, so we have to allow the web server user write access to these folders. Look at the httpd.conf (Apache web server configuration) file and see the user and group used to run Apache. Usually the user and group is *nobody*, so I will use it in my example. Let's say we have the document root of our web server in /www/htdocs. We need to set the file permissions of /www/htdocs/templates_c and /www/htdocs/cache to allow write access for user *nobody*.

```
chown nobody:nobody /www/htdocs/templates_c
chown nobody:nobody /www/htdocs/cache
chmod 770 /www/hdocs/templates_c
chmod 770 /www/htdocs/cache
```

Step 4: Verifying the Installation

To make sure the installation works, copy the demo folder from the Smarty distribution root to the document root of your web server (for example, c:\Apache2\htdocs), edit the index.php file to make sure you have require('smarty.class.php'); and type http://localhost/demo/index.php in your web browser. You should see a demo page with some of Smarty's capabilities and the debugging console. Make sure your browser allows pop-ups.

Smarty Development Versions on CVS

By the way, if you want to play with features in development for future versions of Smarty, then the PHP CVS server hosts the latest version of Smarty (the unstable one) and most of the old releases. CVS can be downloaded from `http://ccvs.cvshome.org/servlets/ProjectDocumentList`.

To download Smarty from the PHP CVS server, first you have to login into the server with the command:

```
cvs -d :pserver:cvsread@cvs.php.net:/repository login
```

using `phpfi` as the password.

To download the current Smarty tree just type:

```
cvs -d :pserver:cvsread@cvs.php.net:/repository co smarty
```

or any stable version of Smarty by using the following command:

```
cvs -d :pserver:cvsread@cvs.php.net:/repository co -r smarty_X_Y_Z smarty
```

where x_y_z is the corresponding version number, for instance using `smarty_2_6_10` in the previous command line will download Smarty release 2.6.10 in the `smarty` folder.

Note that using the current Smarty distribution from the PHP CVS server in production is not recommended at all. It is an unstable version used for development and if you want to use Smarty for building websites you should use the latest stable version.

Upgrading a Smarty Site

Smarty is backward compatible, so when you need to upgrade a Smarty site all you need to do is:

- Get the latest Smarty distribution as described in Step 1 earlier.
- Replace the old content of the `libs` folder where you installed it with the content of the `libs` from the new distribution's root.
- Make sure you don't have the old file `smarty.class.php` in any other PHP include path.

Summary

In this chapter, you learned that using multi-tier software architecture makes our life easier. Smarty's objective is to separate the Business Logic from the Application Logic. Smarty is fast and secure because of the way templates are parsed, which is *template compiling*. It has prefilters, postfilters, and output filters which give the programmer complete control of template output and content. By creating resource handles, you can use templates from any source that you can access with PHP. Smarty has a plug-in architecture so you can use plug-ins for most of its functionality. It also includes a very powerful debugging tool. You also learned how to install Smarty on Windows and Linux.

2
Smarty Site Architecture

It has been a long time since websites have moved on from being simple HTML pages with no frames, no dynamic content, and only a few words about something. Nowadays, building a competitive website is a challenging process for those involved, no different than building most software applications.

Generally speaking, architecture is the fundamental organization of a system. Software architecture consists of defining:

- Software elements for the application
- Relationships between elements
- Relationships between software elements and the environment
- The evolution of the application
- The principles that govern the application

In many ways, software architecture is just like building architecture. You must define the elements used to build the building, how to attach them together, how the building will stand the environment conditions, the order of putting one element over another, and how to use the building.

I know this book is intended to be a tutorial for Smarty, but in order to move deep into Smarty you must understand the process of building a website. Defining architecture for the site gives you a skeleton of the site, emphasizing a clear definition of the structure and the relationship between the components used to fulfill the purpose of the website, and allows you to easily manage your project's resources and timelines. Dividing your project into components allows you to work with more programmers and more designers, gluing these components together at the end of the project. Software architecture implements a clear separation of concerns at most of the functionalities of the application.

In Chapter 1 we discussed using three-tier software architecture for most web projects and we saw how it facilitates separation of the programmer's part from the designer's part. Let's look at *Separation of Concerns* in detail.

Separation of Concerns

The term was introduced by Professor E.W. Dijkstra in his book *A Discipline of Programming* published in 1976 and became one of the most important principles in software engineering.

The concept states that any given problem involves a number of concerns, which should be identified, separated and implemented as separately as possible. This concept promotes modular design, as every feature of the application is written separately.

What Does Concern Mean?

Despite the fact that using Separation of Concerns is a commonly agreed necessity, there is no clear definition of a concern. Generally speaking, a concern is a problem that a program tries to solve. In a website some concerns can be sending emails, creating a shopping basket, creating customer review functionality, and so on. A concern can be seen as a particular goal, concept, or area of interest.

Procedural programming languages allow Separation of Concerns through functions or procedures. In procedural programming, a concern can be modeled as program (functions along with data structures) or as a function within a program.

In **OOP** (Object-Oriented Programming), separated concerns are modeled as objects and classes, while **AOP** (Aspect-Oriented Programming) extends the concept with non-functional properties like memory management, persistency, and synchronization.

While Smarty provides functions like procedural programming languages, the best way to separate concerns using Smarty is to write plug-ins for all major functionalities of the site. Smarty plug-ins are in fact functions that are loaded on demand, but it's a very useful technique to make your site modular and for code reusability.

A Problem-Solving Perspective

The process of building a web page, or any software, is a process of finding a solution to meet the requirements for the page (or software).

```
Requirements -> Website
```

This is the normal process of building a website. From a problem-solving perspective, this gets translated to:

```
Requirements -> Solution
```

Requirements need to be transcribed into problems:

```
Requirements -> Problems -> Solution
```

In practice, analysts have to express the requirements in the right problems in order to find appropriate solutions.

The solution can be defined as a set of abstractions with a set of relations among these abstractions. Therefore, we can say that the solution is a union of two sets:

```
Solution = (Abstractions , Relations)
```

Thus, we can define a *concern* as being a *solution abstraction that is relevant for a given problem.*

Cross-cutting Concerns

Concerns that are not related to core functionality of the application, but are needed to run the application are called cross-cutting concerns. In the problem-solving perspective, relations between abstractions of the solution can help identify cross-cutting concerns.

For example, authentication, logging, and sending emails are the most used cross-cutting concerns in software applications. Cross-cutting concerns must be identified for any application and implemented in such a way that you can reuse the code without rewriting it.

Although you may be tempted to copy and paste, let's say the authentication code in many web pages for the same site, it's more efficient to separate this concern and implement it such that it can be accessed by all the modules. Isolating cross-cutting concerns is the goal of AOP (Aspect-Oriented Programming).

PHP, being a structured programming language (like C for example) can separate concerns through functions. However, you can identify cross-cutting concerns and code them as functions in PHP scripts, then include them in the scripts you need.

Using Smarty, you can identify cross-cutting concerns and implement them as plug-ins. With this, we can truly say, "Developing software using PHP and Smarty allows a clear implementation of Separation of Concerns."

Roles Involved in Building and Maintaining a Website

We are going to review the processes of building and maintaining websites from a project-management point of view.

Firstly, we need a project manager. If there's no one qualified for the job, pick the most experienced person in the team, or, if it's a solo show, you will be the project manager and the web programmer. However, I will try to explain how a professional team works on the project.

The **Customer** is the one who establishes the requirements. Actually, *requirements* is not the appropriate word to use here because it simply represents the customer's desires. Most customers have no idea about the process or technologies in building a website, so they can only express their desires or their needs. This is done at first in a friendly conversation with the project manager who will give an approximate final price.

Analysts are the next to talk to the customer. They will discuss customer needs in more detail in order to express the requirements in a more appropriate way. They also try to establish the structure of the content so they can build a database. The analysts' job is concluded after they come up with a document with the functionality of the site and the database tables and relations.

> Since most websites are database interfaces, the core of the application needs to be very well designed and implemented. Analysts play one of the most important parts, because a complete analysis and a smart database design will guarantee more than 90% the success of the site.

The **Project Manager** establishes timelines and prices for the project, and then signs a contract with the customer if he or she agrees with the analysis, the timelines, and the budget. He or she will assign functionalities to programmers and pick a designer.

The **Designer** creates a few layouts and shows them to the customer. He or she will agree with the customer on the website design.

Meanwhile, the **Programmers** start coding the parts of the application they are assigned. They work with the designer to establish the variables' names.

When the site is ready, the customer tests the functionality according to the analysis. This is usually done on a testing platform. The project manager then must propose a hosting solution. If it's an *in-house* hosting solution he or she must assign a **System Administrator** to handle the installation, the security of the system, and remote tools for programmers and designers.

The website must contain tools for content administration. This way, the customer will manage the content of the site him- or herself so there will be no further need for the programmers or designers on this project, unless the customer decides he or she wants changes in business logic or in presentation.

Website maintenance will be the system administrator's responsibility.

Starting a Smarty Project

We are about to start a Smarty project right now, so I will try to explain a little about the process. First of all, I will try to make the explanation as general as I can, but the project itself will be built on Windows with Apache and PHP 5. If you want to work on Linux, you will have to change some of the things that will follow.

The first step is to choose a text editor. To be honest, my favorite text editors are Notepad in Windows and Joe in Linux, but you should use whatever text editor you feel most comfortable with.

This example will be a short one just to get acquainted with Smarty and the three-tier architecture. We will build a website containing a short list of books by Packt.

Directory Structure

After we have installed Apache, PHP, and Smarty as described in Chapter 1, we need a document root for our project. Let's create a folder, for example `mycode`, in the folder at which the `DocumentRoot` directive found in the `httpd.conf` file of your Apache web server points.

Next, we need to create the templates, template compilation, configuration, and cache folders, which by default are named `templates`, `templates_c`, `configs`, and `cache`. We will create these in the `mycode` folder. The `.php` files will be stored in the `mycode` folder itself. We also need to copy the `libs` folder in your Smarty installation to the `mycode` folder.

Securing our Smarty Project

In my experience, I have noticed that a lot of people who work with Smarty or other template engines don't realize the importance of the fact that their code is intended to be for their eyes only. While .php files are configured in Apache as applications and they are passed to the PHP interpreter when accessed from the Web, templates file with the .tpl extension are not. In Linux, chmod can do a good job with the Smarty folders, but it can cause problems when a designer uploads the files via FTP or HTTP.

Since we named the Smarty folders like their defaults, if we put a file with the .tpl extension in the templates folder (for example, index.tpl), if you write in your web browser address box http://localhost/templates/index.tpl you can see the file with the actual code in it.

Since everything is done internally by Smarty and PHP, there is no need for the web user to access files in any Smarty directory (even if the compilation directory contains PHP files, they are never addressed directly from the Web). Considering these facts, I think that the best way to secure the project is to deny everyone except the *localhost* access to Smarty folders from the Web.

The Data Access Layer

For this example, I took some information about four books from the Packt Publishing website and stored them in a file. I also downloaded the book covers and stored them in a new folder called images, which is within our mycode folder.

In the mycode folder, let's create a file named data.txt with the following information (the file is available in the code download):

```
Title=> Building Websites with VB.NET and DotNetNuke 3.0
Image=> 1904811272.jpg
Author=> Daniel N. Egan
Description=> A practical guide to creating and maintaining your own website
with DotNetNuke, the free, open source evolution of Microsoft's IBuySpy Portal
Year=> 2005
Price=> 39.99

Title=> SSL VPN : Understanding, evaluating and planning secure, web-based
remote access
Image=> 1904811078.jpg
Author=> Joseph Steinberg, Tim Speed, Simon Jenner
Description=> A comprehensive overview of SSL VPN technologies and design
strategies
Year=> 2005
Price=> 49.99

Title=> Windows Server 2003 Active Directory Design and Implementation=>
Creating, Migrating, and Merging Networks
Image=> 1904811086.jpg
Author=> John Savill
Description=> A unique, scenario-based approach to selecting and implementing
the best Active Directory design for your environment
Year=> 2005
Price=> 59.99

Title=> Building Websites with the ASP.NET Community Starter Kit
Image=> 1904811000.jpg
Author=> Cristian Darie, K. Scott Allen
```

```
Description=> A comprehensive guide to understanding, implementing, and
extending the powerful and freely available application from Microsoft
Year=> 2004
Price=> 44.99
```

We will use a file to store our data to show that any change in the way we store data will not affect the business logic layer and the presentation layer.

Next step is to retrieve the data from data.txt. For this, we create a file named get_data.php in the mycode folder with the following content:

```php
<?php

class books {

//public

public $title = array();
public $image = array();
public $author = array();
public $description = array();
public $year = array ();
public $price = array();

// private

private $filename = "data.txt";

//class constructor

function __construct()
{

 //get the lines as an array

  $i=-1;
  $lines = file($this->filename);

// strip "\n" at the end of each array
// get each variable in an array

  foreach ( $lines as $line) {

    if (strlen($line) > 2) {

    $line = rtrim($line);

    list($what, $content) = explode("=> ", $line);

    if ($what == "Title") {
        $i++;
        $this->title[$i]=$content;
        }
    elseif ($what == "Image") {
        $this->image[$i]=$content;
        }
    elseif ($what == "Author") {
        $this->author[$i]=$content;
        }
    elseif ($what == "Description") {
        $this->description[$i]=$content;
        }
    elseif ($what == "Year") {
        $this->year[$i]=$content;
        }
    elseif ($what == "Price") {
        $this->price[$i]=$content;
```

```
        };
         };
     };
} // end constructor
} // end GetData
```

How it Works

The class books has the public variables $title, $image, $author, $description, $year, and $price as arrays, and a private variable called $filename, which stores the name and path of our data file.

When the class is constructed, the constructor function will first read every line from the data file into an array of strings called $lines. For each string representing a line in the data file that has a length bigger than two (so avoiding the blank lines), we will strip the blanks and the end-of-line characters at the end of the string with the rtrim() function.

Then, we will separate the string in two different strings, one named $what and other $content, the first one representing what's on the left of the => characters and the second one what's on the right. After that, we will compare the content of the $what variable to store the data from the $content variable in one of the public arrays of the class (for example, $title[0] will be Building Websites with VB.NET and DotNetNuke 3.0).

> At the Data Access Layer we retrieve the data from the database. In this case, the database is a file. Later, if we want to use a MySQL database with a table named books with the columns title, image, author, description, year, and price, the constructor of the class will get the public variables with a SELECT statement (for example, SELECT title, image, author, description, year, price FROM books).

The Business Logic Layer

After the data is retrieved at the Data Access Layer, the Business Logic Layer is responsible for data validation from the business point of view. In this example, we will apply a ten percent discount for the books published in 2005 and a twenty percent discount for books published in 2004. For this, we need to create a file in the mycode folder named books.php as shown:

```php
<?php

class bo_books {

//public

public $title = array();
public $image = array();
public $author = array();
public $description = array();
public $year = array ();
public $price = array();
public $discount = array();
public $discounted = array();

//private

protected $DataObject;
```

```
function __construct()
{

  $this->DataObject = new books();

}

public function apply_discount()
{

  $this->title = $this->DataObject->title;
  $this->image = $this->DataObject->image;
  $this->author = $this->DataObject->author;
  $this->description = $this->DataObject->description;
  $this->year = $this->DataObject->year;
  $this->price = $this->DataObject->price;

  $j = 0;

  foreach($this->year as $year)
  {

    if ($this->year[$j] == '2004')
        $this->discount[$j] = '20';

    elseif ($this->year[$j] == '2005')
        $this->discount[$j] = '10';

    $this->discounted[$j] = intval($this->price[$j] *
                                  (100 - $this->discount[$j])  ) / 100 ;

    $j++;

  };

} // end function apply_discount()

} // end class bo_books
```

How it Works

The class bo_books is used to pass the data to the Presentation Layer after business logic is used on the data retrieved at the Data Access Layer. It has the same public variables as the books class from get_data.php plus arrays called $discount and $discounted, which represent the discount applied for each book and the price after the discount. The class has a private variable called $DataObject in which the data is retrieved from the Data Access Layer.

The constructor initializes the $DataObject variable as a new books class object and will have the public variables retrieved from the data file.

The public function apply_discount() will copy the content of each public variable from the $DataObject class into the public variables of the current class. After that, it will compare each book's year with the values 2004 and 2005 and assign a discount for each book in the array named $discount.

The discounted price is calculated in the $discounted array:

```
$this->discounted[$j] = intval($this->price[$j] *
                              (100 - $this->discount[$j])  ) / 100 ;
```

The Presentation Layer

First, we need to pass the variables from the Business Logic Layer to the Presentation Layer. In the mycode folder, create a file named index.php like this:

```php
<?php

require("libs/Smarty.class.php");
require_once("get_data.php");
require_once("books.php");

$book = new bo_books();
$book->apply_discount();

$smarty = new Smarty;

$smarty->assign("book",$book);

$smarty->display('index.tpl');

?>
```

Next, we will create an index.tpl file in the templates folder, like this:

```html
<html>
<head> <title> Site Architecture Example </title>
</head>

<body>

<table border="0" width="100%">
  <tr>
    <td align="left">
      <a href="http://www.packtpub.com">
       <img src="images\Packt.png" border="0">
      </a>
      <img src="images\focused.gif">
    </td>
    <td>
    <h1> Chapter 2 Example </h1>
    </td>
  </tr>
</table>

<br>
Here are the books in a two-column table :
<br> <br>

<table border="1" width="100%">

{section name=tbl loop=$book->title}

 {if %tbl.index% is not odd}

 <tr>
 {/if}

 <td align="left">
  <table>
   <tr>
    <td>
      <img src="images\{$book->image[tbl]}" width="220">
    </td>
```

```
        <td valign="top">
          <font size=+1><b> {$book->title[tbl]} </b></font><br>
          <font size=-1 color=blue><b>  {$book->author[tbl]} </b></font><br>
          {$book->description[tbl]} <br>
          Year: {$book->year[tbl]} <br>
          <font size=-1>Cover Price: <s>${$book->price[tbl]}</s></font> <br>
          Our Price: ${$book->discounted[tbl]}
          <font color=red> save {$book->discount[tbl]} % </font>
        </td>
      </tr>
    </table>
  </td>

  {if %tbl.index% is odd}

  </tr>
  {/if}

{/section}

</table>

</body>

</html>
```

How it Works

Being the index file, `index.php` will be the PHP script that will be executed first. It will first load the Smarty library using `require("libs/Smarty.class.php");` and then load the other PHP files described above. This will load the code of the books and bo_books classes.

Next, we create a variable named $book of bo_books class type: `$book = new bo_books()`. The constructor of bo_books will load the data from the Data Access Layer in its private `$DataObject` variable. Next, we want to have all the data about the books from the Data Access Layer in our $book variable and apply the discounts from the Business Logic Layer. This is done by the `apply_discount()` public function of the bo_books class: `$book->apply_discount()`.

Now we have all the data extracted from our data file at the Data Access Layer with logic performed on it by the Business Logic Layer and we want to display it, so we pass the data to the templates: `$smarty->assign("book",$book);`. Next we display the template `index.tpl` using `$smarty->display('index.tpl');`.

The template `index.tpl` is a Smarty template, using which we display our data. It begins just like an HTML file and may contain any HTML tags. At the top of the page we print the Packt logo with a link to Packt's website, and the page title as a heading, all in a two-column table using HTML tags.

Next we create a section loop to generate a table's rows and columns and to print the content: `{section name=tbl loop=$book->title}`. If the `tbl.index` is not odd we will begin a new row, then we print our data, and if the `tbl.index` is odd, after we print the data we print the row's closing tag (`</tr>`).

In every cell of the table we print another table containing the book's image on the left and facts on the right.

The Result

We have obtained a web page that looks like this:

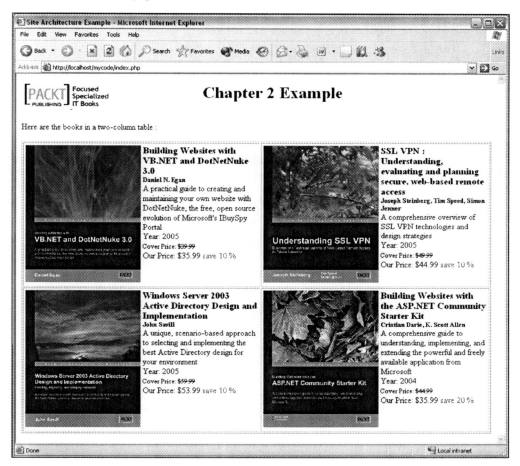

At the centre of this project lies the database, which is a file in our case. This can be any type of database and can be changed at any time.

Above the database there's the Data Access Layer, which consists in our example in the books class contained in the get_data.php file. The class extracts the data from the database so that it can be used by the Business Logic Layer.

The Business Logic Layer is responsible for data validation and manipulation from the business point of view. In our example, the class bo_books gets the data from the Data Access Layer and applies a discount of 10% for the books published in 2005 and a discount of 20% for the ones published in 2004. If we want to change the discounts, all we need to do is modify the apply_discount() function of the class, so all business logic is separated here from data access and presentation.

After our data is extracted from the database and passed through the Business Logic Layer, we must create the presentation part of our project. This is done by creating templates and shows the data just the way we want, independently from the way data gets extracted or any business logic is performed on the data. In our example we see how Smarty supports looping with a small section loop. We will see more looping techniques later in this book.

The purpose of this project was to get familiar with three-tier architecture and how to separate layers.

Summary

In this chapter, you learnt how using software architecture makes your life easier. We also looked at what the *Separation of Concerns* concept is, why it is so widely used and how we should see the *Separation of Concerns* from a problem-solving perspective. We also looked at the roles played by various people involved in a Smarty project and each one's responsibilities. You learned how to start a Smarty Project and about its folders and security. We also studied the various layers of a smarty project:The Data Access Layer, the Business Logic Layer and the Presentation Layer. By the end of this chapter you should have a small project with Smarty and PHP 5 that uses three-tier software architecture.

3

What Designers Need to Know

In the previous chapters you learned about the basic concepts and setting up of Smarty. As a Smarty developer, you have to understand some basic procedures and know how. This chapter will guide you through the necessary steps to kick start template designing. Before starting template design, you should always be aware of the main objective of Smarty. Let me repeat again for you that the main goal of Smarty is to separate the presentation layer from business logic. This chapter will show you the best way to develop templates while keeping this goal in perspective, and at the same time satisfying your programmers, helping you to co-operate with them, minimizing their task, and increasing the reusability of your final output.

One more thing you should be aware of is that you shouldn't mix up identities. Most often, the designers are to some extent programmers and vice versa. While designing you must totally forget that you are also a programmer and look at things only from a designer's perspective. If you mix up your identities, there will be a great risk of non-standard designs.

Development Team Problems: Common Scenarios

Do you remember those days when you hard coded your business logic into your HTML pages? To some developers, this embedding capability brought an extra level of satisfaction. You designed (let's read *hard coded*—we are still in your old days) a lot of pages for your extremely beautiful site and delivered it to the customer. Only to be faced with problems when even a small change needed to be made to the site. Now let's look at common problems faced during those days by designers, managers, and developers, and their possible solutions (with and without Smarty):

- **Designer's Problem:**
    - **Problem**: After using your solution for some days, the customer requires a small change in site layout. The change is required within a very short time and there is no way you can extend the deadline or avoid it.
    - **Solution without using Smarty**: In this situation, you will go to your desk, won't sleep for some nights and will change all those hard-coded pages by manually modifying them one by one. Are you scared that something similar might happen again? Undoubtedly, you are. Maybe you could tackle it this time, but when you have hundreds of such pages, it will be very different.

- o **Solution using Smarty**: Open your Smarty templates, perform the necessary change, and upload it to your server. You don't have to worry about processed data and business logic. Moreover, you needn't worry about searching through a lot of gibberish code and spending a lot of time and effort changing it.

- **Manager/Developer's Problem**:
  - o **Problem**: You are the manager of this company. You need to modify your existing site's appearance and suddenly you find that the programmer who hard coded this site has quit a few days ago.
  - o **Solution without using Smarty**: You will hire another programmer who will read the previous code, figure out the portions to change and then make the changes. It may sound easy but actually, it's not. Reading code written by another programmer is a very tough job. Furthermore, if your previous programmer didn't document the coding, it will create bigger complications.
  - o **Solution using Smarty**: Ask your Smarty template designer to perform necessary changes and save it. There is a chance that you may not even need to look at your inner business logic and codes.

Do these scenarios make any sense to you? Well, these two scenarios are enough to illustrate the situation of a designer and a manager. Which one do you relate to? This chapter and the upcoming chapters will help you to solve problems like these in a more effective way by using the Smarty templating engine.

Roles of a Template Designer and a Programmer

There are at least two significant players in a web application development team. They are the designers and coders. They each have distinct roles but must work together to make this web application successful, easy to maintain, and easy to extend. Firstly, let's go through the detailed role of a designer.

- **Separate the presentation layer**: As a designer, your primary job is to completely separate the presentation code from your business logic. You must ensure that this separation will be usable and optimized.

- **Figure out fixed parts and dynamic parts**: Before you start designing, you must figure out which parts will be dynamic and which parts will be static.

- **Figure out reusable parts and make best use of them**: Separate your template into components (like a header, navigation bar, body, footer, and so on) and ensure integrity between them.

- **Collaborate with programmers**: See what parameters programmers give you and how you can use them. If you need something more or find something that is lacking, you should immediately inform them.

- **Design plug-ins and modifiers if necessary**: If you are not familiar with extending Smarty (though it's in some ways a programmer's job; but it may be considered as a big plus point if you are familiar with it and will give you an extra facility), at least inform the programmers in your team that you need a special functionality that could be accomplished by plug-ins or modifiers.

The programmer's role is beyond the scope of this chapter. However, for the sake of simplicity let's see the programmer's basic role.

- Implement business logics.
- Assign necessary data to variables and document it. Documenting is a best practice and you should always maintain it.
- Work in close contact with designers and supply them with whatever they need.
- Develop plug-ins if needed.

Since you now have a clear understanding about your role as designer, let's go through every important point you have to take care of.

Definitions and Concepts for Designers

Just opening your editor and writing Smarty tags with variables supplied by programmers will never make you a top designer. As a designer, you should be familiar with these terms and processes before you start.

Caching: This is the process of temporarily storing the output and using it from this storage when necessary. Caching increases Smarty's performance greatly as it avoids extra calculation for a Smarty template and thus reduces the script execution time. Caching gives Smarty an edge over other template engines.

Optimization: This is the process of removing overload from your browser and allowing your template to work well with minimal memory. Simply reducing the size of your page is not optimization. You should also take care of extra images and extra HTML code for your design. For example, the navigation bar is a part of website that hardly changes itself dynamically page by page. Hence, you should leave it as a separate component and ask your programmer to cache it.

Stylesheet (Cascading Style Sheets or CSS): This is a language for formatting the output of HTML tags. As a designer, you must have a strong grounding in stylesheets. In older days, people used <table> to design their site. These days, they use <div> instead. With <div> and CSS you have full control over the placement of objects and can design liquid layouts according to your need. <div> and CSS give you maximum control over your website and increase the reusability of your template components. In addition, optimized CSS upgrades your site for faster loading and less bandwidth consumption. CSS also allows you to use shorthand style, which is an extra benefit.

Debugging: This is the process of eliminating the errors, bugs, and bad code that give a wrong result. As a designer, you should be capable of debugging your templates. Smarty has its own debug capability in the form of a debug console. While designing, you will realize that most errors occur when your programmers supply you with a lot of data using nested arrays and you have to iterate through them to output a fantastic result. If any error occurs, you have to check and recheck your template to find out where the error occurred. The Smarty debug console helps you to analyze instantly what your programmers supplied you and identify the parameter(s) that caused the error. Smarty lets you debug your template as intuitively and simply as possible.

JavaScript: You can embed JavaScript in your templates. However, for the sake of optimization, separate the JavaScript into another file and link to that file with the `<script>` tag. This will optimize your template and the browser will load this JavaScript file from cache and not from the server. Take extra care while embedding JavaScript in your template to avoid compile-time bugs.

Object-Oriented Programming (OOP): As I have already mentioned, if you have some basic programming knowledge, it will help you in template design. You may ask "How?" Well, Smarty is a templating engine that allows your programmer to pass arrays and nested arrays, which you can access in three styles, normal *index* style, *associative* style, or *high-level object-oriented* style. However, that's not where your knowledge about OOP helps you. You will be surprised to know that Smarty allows programmers to pass an entire object (a class as an object), which you can handle in your template. The benefit of this is that you can access attributes and methods of this object inside your template. You can even pass parameters from your template to that object.

Plug-ins and Modifiers: A designer must know what modifiers and plug-ins are. These are simple functions that work with the Smarty engine as embedded objects. Smarty lacks some features in order to maintain its simplicity and extensibility, but it gives you full control over extending it. If you ever feel that you need to do some special processing with your variable, content, or the whole template then you can ask the programmers to develop a plug-in or modifier to meet your requirement. We will go through the detail of extending Smarty later in this book. Nevertheless, let's understand what plug-ins and modifiers are. A plug-in is a special function that allows you to modify a whole block of content inside a template or to add a complete new tag to your Smarty engine. Modifiers are functions that simply modify the variable content.

Basic programming knowledge: Besides being a templating engine, Smarty is also a new language for templating. It has all the key features of a programming language. Hence, Smarty is not very easy and you should spend some studying it. If basic concepts of programming like logic development, loops, conditional flow, and array manipulation are totally unknown to you, please study them carefully. A template, unlike WYSIWYG HTML design, requires experience, regular practice, and foresight.

Concept of Reusability and Components

Reusability is a common concept that a Smarty template designer can benefit from. Firstly, let's see what reusability is. It is the process of designing a component or object in such a way that you can use it repeatedly in different projects either as it is or with a simple modification. Here, by components, we mean important, individual parts of your web page.

Let us assume you design a template that represents an entire page and contains a menu bar, header, footer, body, banner rotator, calendar, news rotator, and so on. A template *can* contain many components in a single page. However, this kind of template wouldn't be standard in the context of modern web design style, and as such, is not *optimized*. The following code snippet is a typical example of such a non-structured but working template:

```
<HTML>
    <body>
        {code for banner}
        {code for menu bar}
        {code for body}  //inside this there are {code for news
                            rotator} and {code for advertisement}
        {code for footer}
    </body>
</HTML>
```

Now let's design another page with a slight modification. You will again copy and paste most of the page and change the <body> part, give your template to another designer in your team and tell him or her to design a third page with a slight modification in the news rotator. He or she will have to study your whole template and understand which portion of your template is responsible for news rotation. If your template is filled with many business logic sections, it's a bit of a hassle for him or her. How can you help your other programmers not to copy and paste every component in their every template? Split them up into components. Design separate templates for each section and integrate them in your final template. Look at the structure below:

```
{include your header template}
{include your menu bar template}
{include your body template}
{include your footer template}
```

Moreover, inside your body template just include your {news rotator template} and {advertisement template}. What benefit do you get if you follow this style? Let's see.

- When you need something to be changed, just change the component. No need to spend extra time on studying, and aligning the complete template code.

- More structured to understand.

- Each component is individually reusable. Suppose one of your co-developers needs just the news rotator part; he or she can simply include your news rotator component.

- This will help you while designing by increasing concentration on each part.

These are more or less all the benefits, but the most important benefit is reusability. Don't overlook component separation—it will help you and your team to save a lot of time while modifying and extending your site.

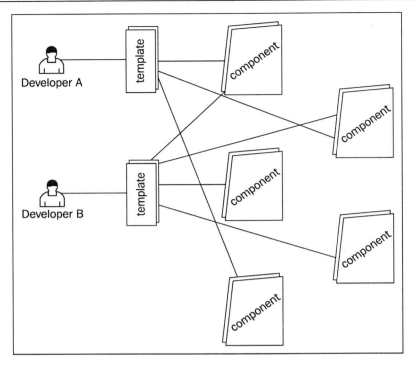

The diagram above clearly illustrates how you can reuse your components in different templates. Developer A developed a template that uses three components and Developer B developed a template that uses four components. Both templates share two components between them. If there are a huge number of templates, then this process will definitely save your many nights' sleep.

However, there is a pitfall in this style. If you follow this style, you need to assign only one person for a single component. It's not a good practice to have more than one person designing a single component.

Splitting into Components

You already have some idea of splitting a web page into components. It will help if we take a closer look before proceeding further. Let's see components in action. Here is a screenshot of the Packt website.

Assuming this is a sample page of your site, let's define which could be the components. Can you figure out how many components we can divide the page into? Let's start one by one.

- Banner with embedded menu bar
- Left Navigation Panel
  - A small navigation menu
  - A search box with a newsletter subscription box
  - News rotator
- Body
  - General heading
  - Recent book description rotator
- Right Panel
  - Simple News rotator
- Footer

We can split the whole page into these components. Note that there are three news rotators in the page: in the left panel, in the body (as a book description rotator), and in the right panel. Just this single page reuses a news rotator component three times with a different look-and-feel using CSS classes.

Let's look at a typical webpage and the components it usually contains:

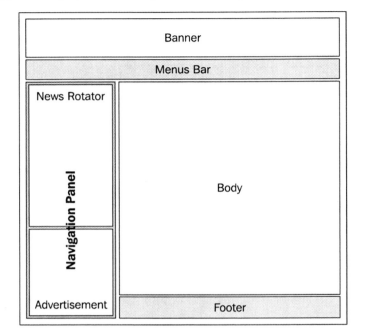

The figure above shows you typical components that are commonly used in a webpage. Whenever you plan to design a template, keep in mind that more or less every page uses these components. Let me clarify content separation a bit more. Let us suppose you have a website where you sell items.

When you're deciding how to split your page into components, it's useful to think about **reusability**. If you design a separate template for each item, then you can use that template every time the item is required on another page. On the other hand, don't overdo your splitting into components so small that you'll never make use of them on their own. Otherwise, you could end up wasting a lot of time on splitting a template into hundreds of tiny components!

Let's go into depth: How should each component look? I am not going to discuss Smarty codes in this chapter, rather pure HTML to show you the basic structure of each component.

If you prefer table-less design then design each component enclosed by the <div> object. We already discussed in brief why table-less design is extensible for designers. If you prefer flexible templating, do it table-less. However, if you use templates for pure reporting, then a table is flexible to manage. Choose whatever suits you best.

How to Design Table-less Layouts?

Table-less design gives you unlimited flexibility and reduces the HTML code on your page, but requires in-depth knowledge of CSS. It saves a lot of time that you would otherwise spend on a table and its cell alignment. In the next example, we will design a very basic table-less page with the usual components.

This is your sample HTML without a table:

```
<body>
<div id="container">
<div id="head">
<div id="header"> <h1>Header</h1> </div>
</div>
<div id="menubar_horizontal"> Menubar </div>
<div id="content">
    <div id="leftpanel">
        <div id="menubar_vertical">Menubar Vertical</div>
        <div id="news">News</div>
    </div>
    <div id="body">Body</div>
</div>
<div id="footer">Footer</div>
</div>
</body>
```

The output will look like this:

Header

Menubar

Menubar Vertical

News

Body

Footer

Now attach the following style sheet to this web page:

```
<style>
div
{
    border: 1px solid #333233;
}
#container
{
    width: 780px;
    margin: auto;
    border: 0px;
}
#head
{
    height: 100px;
}
#header
{
    text-align: center;
    margin-top: 30px;
    border: 0px;
}
```

```
#menubar_horizontal
{
     margin-top: 5px;
     padding: 5px;
     text-align: right;
}
#content
{
     margin-top: 5px;
     padding: 5px;
}
#leftpanel
{
     height: 350px;
     width: 200px;
     padding: 5px;
     float: left;
}
#menubar_vertical, #news
{
     width: 190px;
     margin: auto;
     margin-top: 5px;
     padding: 5px;
}
#menubar_vertical{
     height: 150px;
}
#news
{
     height: 180px;
}
#body{
     left: 210px;
     height: 359px;
     padding: 5px;
}
#footer
{
     margin-top: 5px;
     padding: 5px;
}
</style>
```

The output will now be completely different, as shown in the figure opposite. Without using any tables, you have a well-structured design.

CSS is a very powerful tool. Take a closer look at the CSS code above to get a feel of how it works. The purpose of this example is to show that whenever you write a specific component, it's worth writing it inside a `<div>` tag and then processing it with your cascading style sheets.

You should also correctly identify the fixed and dynamic parts of your site. Any part of your template that is not enclosed by a Smarty tag is fixed. It can only change if somebody comes and edits the template. (A fixed part may be conditional, that is, if a condition is satisfied, a specific fixed part may be displayed—but the content of that part will always be fixed.)

Some dynamic parts, such as Navigation Menus, will only change rarely. It's still best to treat these as dynamic parts. In later chapters, we will see how to use *caching* so that rarely updated sections are not regenerated every time a page is requested. This will make your site faster, although for many sites the difference will not be noticeable.

Handy Built-in Tags

Smarty comes with some handy tags that can reduce your design time to a great extent. These tags are pre-configured to deliver some helpful HTML components. Always try to use them instead of coding your own components.

A short selection of handy plug-ins is HTML_options, HTML_radios, HTML_select_time, HTML_select_date, HTML_table, and textformat. These will be discussed in the next chapter.

Choosing an Editor for Template Design

There are several commercial as well as freeware WYSIWYG or visual editors available for editing HTML as well as templates. Editing some complex templates *demands* that you have a visual editor. Text editors such as Notepad work too, but they aren't very feature rich and don't provide you with the advance templating features available in visual editors. Macromedia Dreamweaver MX (DWMX), a popular commercial visual editor, is probably the most advanced. Let's see some screenshots that show you how to visually edit your template without any Smarty code.

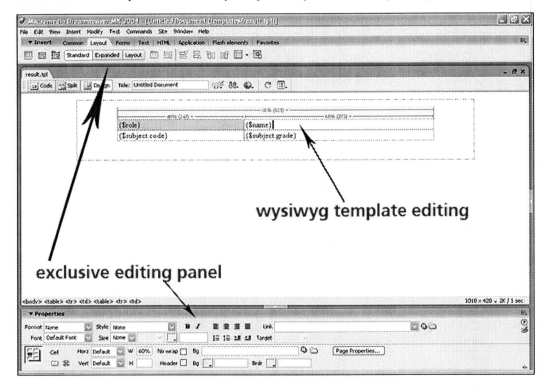

In DWMX you can edit and view your template at the same time, which helps you to place correct tags in their exact position.

Finally, DWMX gives you a rich toolset for different widgets, which will reduce the time for template editing so you can concentrate more on Smarty instead of wasting time in raw HTML.

There is also an extension that allows you to manipulate several Smarty tags inside DWMX. This extension is free of cost but using it requires a bit more knowledge about Smarty. Hence, we are not looking at it in detail. You may visit the website `http://smartydwt.klitsche.org/` for more information about this tool.

There are several other commercial alternatives to DWMX like Microsoft FrontPage, CofeeCup HTML editor, Adobe GoLive, HoTMetaL PRO, and so on.

Note that commercial hi-fi WYSIWYG editors are not mandatory, they are just able to make your life easier while editing templates with their rich toolsets. Some people simply use notepad to develop excellent sites. Before ending this section, just one more editor for you and that is **HTMLGate Free**. This award-winning, WYSIWYG editor is developed by MP Software (`www.mpsoftware.dk`) and is available free of cost.

Collaborating with Programmers

While editing templates you must collaborate with your programmers. Programmers fetch items of data and assign them to variables, which are passed to a designer. As a designer, you must know the structure and contents of these variables. The typical tasks that a designer needs to do are:

- Ask your programmer to document properly the variables, arrays and anything else he or she passes to you.

- Take extra care if the supplied array is associative or indexed, because templating style will be changed in these two cases.

- Always use {debug} in the start of your template to recheck what is supplied to you. As every designer faces problems manipulating arrays and nested arrays, it's better to turn on debugging from the first. Before deployment, just remove this line.

- As I said before, if you need a special functionality in your Smarty template engine, ask programmers in your team to develop it for you. On the other hand, if your programmer develops a plug-in, ask him or her to supply documentation.

- If your programmer supplies an object to you, (classes could be passed to template designers to exclusively access their methods and properties) ask him or her at the very beginning about exposed methods and attributes.

- Always recheck your designed templates with programmers. This synergy will help you to output the best usable template.

Summary

Smarty is as good as a separate language. It gives you full flexibility over designing your templates, but you have to be cautious while doing your job. Don't mess too much with graphics, fonts, or colors. Pay more attention to reusability and component separation. Spend some time in planning before hard coding your template.

Finally, remember that design is an art, so imagine as much as you can—it doesn't matter whether it is impossible or possible—just imagine. Note down your proposals, choose the best feasible one among them and then start designing.

4
Creating a Template

So far you have understood the dos and don'ts for a template designer. Are you waiting to see how templates work in real-world problems and how you can design them to solve your daily needs? This chapter will guide you through real-life problems and their solutions. We will see the basics as well as some interesting templates, but won't look at the code in detail.

Can you imagine scenarios in which Smarty templates would be fruitful? Can you imagine how you can realize your wildest web page designs using Smarty? Not yet? This chapter will help you to tap the full potential of Smarty. Ready? Let's go…

Design Concepts, from HTML to TPL

Smarty templates are written in simple HTML, with embedded Smarty tags. Whatever you can do with an HTML page, you can do with templates. Templates are not pure HTML. They may contain logic as well as some very basic elements of a programming language. Hence, designing them needs a little bit more planning and you may need to study the templating system as well. Previously there were some templating engines that worked using the variable substitution process. This used to work but was a slow process and template designers weren't able to achieve full flexibility using it. Smarty is much faster as it compiles your templates into raw PHP code, executes it and returns pure HTML to end users. Smarty TPL (Template Programming Language) makes the job easy for you. All you have to know are its syntax and usage. Don't worry as the learning curve of Smarty is short. Smarty TPL is a feature-rich language that allows you to solve almost every kind of presentation problem.

In pure HTML, there was nothing dynamic and everything was processed on the client's machine. Server-side languages like PHP solved this problem. They increased the interactivity to a higher level and are doing a fine job. Smarty was introduced to further ease the life of designers and developers. Let's look at how a static HTML website differs from PHP and Smarty TPL.

Every Smarty template contains some functions and variables. These functions are pre-programmed to perform various actions. Using variables, you can *talk* to your programmers. Programmers usually supply data in PHP variables and you have to process them with Smarty functions and variables. Let's see the following examples.

```html
<html>
<body>
<table width="80%"  border="1" cellspacing="0" cellpadding="2">
   <tr>
      <td width="38%" bgcolor="#CCCCCC" ><strong>Profile of
Mortuza</strong></td>
      <td width="62%"> </td>
   </tr>
   <tr>
      <td><strong>Name : </strong></td>
      <td>Mortuza Morshed </td>
   </tr>
   <tr>
      <td>Born</td>
      <td>1980</td>
   </tr>
   <tr>
      <td>Blood Group </td>
      <td>O (+ve) </td>
   </tr>
   <tr>
      <td>Email</td>
      <td>mortuzamorshed@somedomain.com</td>
   </tr>
</table>
<br>
<table width="80%"  border="1" cellspacing="0" cellpadding="2">
   <tr>
      <td width="38%" bgcolor="#CCCCCC" ><strong>Profile of Ayesha
</strong></td>
      <td width="62%"> </td>
   </tr>
   <tr>
      <td><strong>Name : </strong></td>
      <td>Ayesha Siddika</td>
   </tr>
   <tr>
      <td>Born : </td>
      <td>1979</td>
   </tr>
   <tr>
      <td>Blood Group : </td>
      <td>B (+ve) </td>
   </tr>
   <tr>
      <td>Email : </td>
      <td>ayeshasiddika@somedomain.com</td>
   </tr>
</table>
</body>
</html>
```

Profile of Mortuza	
Name :	Mortuza Morshed
Born	1980
Blood Group	O (+ve)
Email	mortuzamorshed@somedomain.com

Profile of Ayesha	
Name :	Ayesha Siddika
Born :	1979
Blood Group :	B (+ve)
Email :	ayeshasiddika@somedomain.com

This is a typical example to display two profiles. You were lucky to get only two. If there were hundreds or thousands, you would have to write each of them in static HTML form. Let's see how Smarty simplifies this problem, provided you have all this data stored in a database. Following is a sample Smarty template for this:

profiles.tpl

```
<body>
{foreach item=student from=$students}
<table width="80%"  border="1" cellspacing="0" cellpadding="4">
  <tr>
    <td width="38%" bgcolor="#CCCCCC">
    <strong>Profile of {$student.nick}</strong></td>
    <td width="62%"> </td>
  </tr>
  <tr>
    <td>Name : </td>
    <td>{$student.name}</td>
  </tr>
  <tr>
    <td>Born</td>
    <td>{$student.born}</td>
  </tr>
  <tr>
    <td>Blood Group </td>
    <td>{$student.blood_grp}</td>
  </tr>
  <tr>
    <td>Email</td>
    <td>{student.email}</td>
  </tr>
</table><br/>
{/foreach}
</body>
```

Note that this is simple HTML code with some embedded Smarty variables. So what do these variables contain and how are they populated? Let's take a look at the following PHP script, which populates and displays variables using the Smarty template engine:

profiles.php

```
<?
include("libs/smarty.class.php");
$smarty = new Smarty ();

[.. your database connection done here ..]

$result = mysql_query("SELECT nick, name, born, blood_grp, email
                        FROM students st
                        LIMIT 10
                      "); //your sql
$students = array(); //just an empty array
while ($row = mysql_fetch_assoc($result))
{
    $students[] = $row; //append the whole $row array in $students
}

$smarty->assign("students",$students); //assign
$smarty->display("profiles.tpl"); //compile and render the output
?>
```

This PHP script simply fetches data from a table *students* into an array, appends it to a collection array ($students) and finally assigns it to the Smarty engine. Next, it calls the display() method with the template file name as a parameter. The display() method renders your template with these variables and returns the output to your browser.

Now run this script. What do you see? This is the same output as your static HTML produced. It doesn't matter whether your database has hundreds or thousands or more records. They will all be displayed without a single change in business logic or template code.

Take a look at the template code profiles.tpl, which has some portions highlighted. These are the Smarty functions and variables. Variables are managed by the PHP script written by programmers. A designer's job is to use them where they need to be used.

Introduction to Smarty Variables

In general, variables are containers that store a chunk of data. Smarty variables are no different but in most cases they are populated using a PHP script. While naming the variables, follow the same convention as you did in PHP. For example, here are some rules:

- Don't start with a numerical character
- Avoid using the name of any reserved variable of PHP (like $_POST or $_SERVER)
- Give it a meaningful name (for the sake of simplicity)
- Start it with a $ sign

Moreover all Smarty variables must be enclosed with braces {}. These are the basic conventions for naming Smarty variables. Let's see a small template and an example of assigning variables in a script.

sample.tpl

```
<html>
<body>
Hello {$name}, {$greetings}.
</body>
</html>
```

Save this file in your templates folder as `sample.tpl`. In this template, there are two variables named {$name} and {$greetings}. We will now populate these variables using our PHP script.

sample.php

```php
<?php
include("libs/smarty.class.php");
$smarty = new smarty();
$sample_name = "Jamil Ahmed";
$smarty->assign("name", $sample_name);
$smarty->assign("greetings", "Good Morning");
$smarty->display("sample.tpl");
?>
```

Save this file as `sample.php` and run it. You will get the following result:

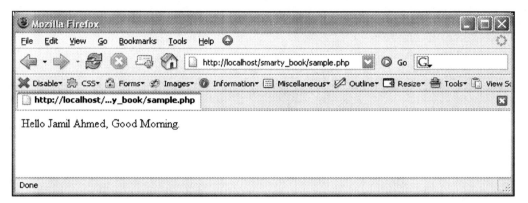

As you can see, Smarty substitutes the template variable {$name} and {$greetings} with data supplied from your PHP script. You can assign variables with the `assign()` method. In the `assign()` method, the first parameter is the name of the Smarty variable and the second parameter is the data you want to assign to it. To assign a variable in the template itself, use the `assign()` function inside your template like this:

```
{assign var = "date" value = "27th September,  2005"}
Today is {$date}
```

This will output **Today is 27th September, 2005**. You don't need to assign any extra data to this {$date} variable. You can assign any data, array and user-defined objects (mainly classes) in a Smarty variable. If you pass an object to your template, you can even access its methods and properties inside your template. Smarty gives you ultimate flexibility while templating. Later in this chapter we will discuss arrays.

Starting Templates

In real-world web development, templates can get much more complicated than this. Smarty templates are great for solving complicated development problems in a simple way. As we have discussed in previous chapters, if you properly plan before starting your template, it will save your time and money.

Before starting your template, make sure you have a solid understanding of the Smarty foundations. Don't leap in after skim-reading this chapter! Paying careful and imaginative attention to the Smarty basics will prove worthwhile.

Templates in real life use arrays in a big way. Arrays in Smarty, like those in other programming languages are just a collection of variables. In PHP, arrays are of two different types, one is a non-associative array where array values have no key, and the other is associative where values are associated with keys. Let's see these two types.

Non-associative Array

```
$students = array("Didar", "Emran", "Hasan", "Deborah", "Shahana");
```

In the above array example, $students is an array where $students[0] is Didar, $students[1] is Emran and so forth. It is the most common style of populating an array but associative arrays have some benefit over non-associative arrays.

Associative Array

```
$students = array(
      "didar" => array("name"=>"Didar Bhuiyan", "roll"=>12)
      "emran" => array("name"=>"Emran Hasan", "roll"=>18)
      "hasan" => array("name"=>"Tanveer Hasan", "roll"=>23));
```

In this array, all items are pointed to by a *key*. For example $students["didar"] is an array with two items, name and roll. So if you want to see what is the *roll number* of *Didar* then you can access it via $students['didar']['roll']. This code is much more readable than something like $students[0][1]. You should try your best to use associative arrays in your templates for the sake of simplicity. In some complex cases, however, non-associative arrays are flexible to manage in Smarty templates.

Now that you have some basic idea about arrays, let's see how to pass arrays to Smarty templates and how to manipulate them.

Passing Arrays to Smarty Templates and Manipulating Them

In this section, we will pass arrays from PHP code to the Smarty templating engine and discuss how to process them. You will find that it is very useful to pass an associative array instead of a non-associative one because you can access each element of this array with a readable name, which in turn, simplifies the code and also increases the extensibility. Let's take a look at this code:

associative_array.php

```
<?
    include_once("libs/smarty.class.php");
    $smarty = new smarty();
    $students = array(
        "didar" => array("name"=>"Didar Bhuiyan","roll"=>12),

        "emran" => array("name"=>"Emran Hasan","roll"=>18),
        "hasan" => array("name"=>"Tanveer Hasan","roll"=>23));
    $smarty->assign("students",$students);
    $smarty->display("associative_array.tpl");
?>
```

54

associative_array.tpl

```
<html>
<body>
<table>
<tr><td>Name</td><td>Roll</td></tr>
{foreach item=student from=$students}
    <tr>
        <td>{$student.name}</td>
        <td>{$student.roll}</td>
    </tr>
    {/foreach}
    </table>
    </body>
</html>
```

Run the associative_array.php file, and you will see output like this:

How is this done for every item in this array? If you look at the code, there is a {foreach} tag, which creates a loop. A loop is a block of code that repeats while a condition is true. Here this loop iterates through every element of the array. When it gets an element, note that it is also an array of a roll and a name item. So we can access them with a dot (.) sign after the array variable. {$student.roll} means the "roll" item of the current array, {$student.name} means the name.

If you pass the array as an object, you can access its elements using OOP-style PHP in your Smarty templates. Let's see how to access them in OOP style.

oop_style.php

```
<?
include_once("libs/smarty.class.php");
class student
{
    var $name;
    var $roll;
}
```

55

```
    $student = new student();
    $student->name = "Arifin";
    $student->roll = "29";

    $smarty = new smarty();

    $smarty->assign("student", $student);
    $smarty->display("oop_style.tpl");
    ?>
```

oop_style.tpl

```
<table>
<tr><td>Name</td><td>Roll</td></tr>
    <tr>
        <td>{$student->name}</td>
        <td>{$student->roll}</td>
</tr>
</table>
```

The only important thing to point out here is the accessing style. Every item is accessed using OOP-style PHP, which means an object followed by an "->" operator.

Template designers, note down how the documentation by programmers can help you in these cases. This documentation helps you to create the loop, to access the array and of course to use the appropriate variable in the correct place. Don't neglect the documentation. Remember that it will save you many sleepless nights.

Basic Templating

We are now going to show you how to develop templates to meet your real-world needs. Templates can be used in multiple places from basic forms to dynamic reports, simple web pages to extremely complex ones. In this section we will show you some great examples of Smarty templating and scripts to manage them.

Templates in the real world are a bit complex. To start, let's gain a basic understanding of logical conditions and loops.

Logical Conditions

Almost all programmers are familiar with logical conditions. Smarty TPL comes with useful logical statements that you can use in your templates. Smarty logic differs in syntax from PHP. In PHP, the scope of if is defined by braces, but in Smarty the scope is defined by an {if}{/if} block. All PHP conditional operators are supported by Smarty {if}. Let's look at the following comparison operator table taken from the Smarty manual:

Qualifier	Alternatives	Syntax Example	Meaning	PHP Equivalent
==	eq	$a eq $b	equals	==
!=	ne, neq	$a neq $b	not equals	!=
>	gt	$a gt $b	greater than	>
<	lt	$a lt $b	less than	<

Qualifier	Alternatives	Syntax Example	Meaning	PHP Equivalent
>=	gte, ge	$a ge $b	greater than or equal	>=
<=	lte, le	$a le $b	less than or equal	<=
===		$a === 0	check for identity	===
!	not	not $a	negation (unary)	!
%	mod	$a mod $b	modulus	%
is [not] div by		$a is not div by 4	divisible by	$a % $b == 0
is [not] even		$a is not even	[not] an even number (unary)	$a % 2 == 0
is [not] even by		$a is not even by $b	grouping level [not] even	($a / $b) % 2 == 0
is [not] odd		$a is not odd	[not] an odd number (unary)	$a % 2 != 0
is [not] odd by		$a is not odd by $b	[not] an odd grouping	($a / $b) % 2 != 0

To define various conditions, Smarty also supports {elseif} and {else}. Let's go through an example to show Smarty {if} {else} {/if} in action.

sample_if.tpl
```
<table>
<tr><td>Name</td><td>Roll</td><td>Grade</td></tr>
    <tr>
        <td>{$student->name}</td>
        <td>{$student->roll}</td>
{if $student.grade='F'}
<td bgcolor='red'>Failed</td>
{else}
<td bgcolor='green'>Passed</td>
{/if}
</tr>
</table>
```

This {if} block, changes the table cell color according to the supplied grade of a student. If the grade is F, it will be shown in a red background. Otherwise, green. You can write multiple conditions using the {if} {elseif} {elseif} {else} {/if} style. In Smarty, you can also implement a nested {if} {/if} block.

Loops

In Smarty, you can perform loops with two different tags. One is {section} and the other is {foreach}. Both of them are significant in different scenarios. {section} is very helpful when programmers supply the arrays in non-associative style. You can traverse through the index of an array. In this chapter you have already seen some examples of {foreach}. We will discuss them a bit more in this section.

section

{section} needs two parameters, name and loop, where name could be anything alphabetical and increases in each iteration. The other required parameter is loop. This is the name of the supplied array variable through which the {section} loops. But how many times does the loop iterate? This depends on the number of items in the supplied array, or anything you specified exclusively. {section} has four more optional parameters. One is start, which determines the initial counter, step is the increment, max is the maximum value that the {section} will loop, and a Boolean parameter show, which determines whether the {section}{/section} block will be displayed or not.

sample_section.tpl

```
{section name=my_loop loop=3}
    I am Looping <br/>
{section}
```

Just note that we didn't supply any array here. If you run this, this will simply print:

I am looping

I am looping

I am looping

sample_section2.tpl

```
<table>
{section name=id loop=$titles}
    <tr>
        <td><tmg src={$images[id]}</td>
        <td>Title: {$titles[id]}<br/>
          Price: {$price[id]}<br/>
            Author: {$authors[id]}</td>
    </tr>
{/section}
```

Let's write a small PHP script that will fetch book data from your database and supply them to your template.

sample_section2.php

```
<?
    #...your mysql connection & smarty initialization goes here
    $result = mysql_query(SELECT title, image, price, author from books LIMIT 20);
    while ($row = mysql_fetch_assoc($result)
    {
        $titles[] = $row['title'];
        $images[] = $row['image'];
        $prices[] = $row['images'];
        $authors[] = $row['author'];
    }
    $smarty->assign("titles",$titles);
    $smarty->assign("images",$images);
    $smarty->assign("prices",$prices);
    $smarty->assign("authors",$authors);

    $smarty->display("sample_section2.tpl");

?>
```

If you run the script then you see the following output:

Just take a look at the code once again and note that the {section} loops with the $titles array. As the id increments, we can use other assigned arrays with this id in the {section} scope. Here, all the supplied arrays are non-associative.

> Though the {section} name increments, you can't display it as {$section_name}. You have to use some built-in properties of the {section} tag.

{section} has some built-in variables that give you extra facility and control its attributes. These are discussed below.

index

index shows you the current loop index of the loop. This is very helpful if you want to display a serial number or if you want to process a particular loop index. It is used as shown here:

```
{section name=id loop=3}
    This is loop index {$smarty.section.id.index}<br/>
{/section}
```

This will output

This is loop index 0

This is loop index 1

This is loop index 2

first

first gives you the first index of the loop. Usually this is zero, but this could be overridden if you specify the starting index by start attribute of {section}. You can use first to initialize if anything needs to be done before the further iterations. For example, you can check this:

```
{if $smarty.section.section_name.first}
<h2>This is Heading</h2>
{else}
do what ever you want
{endif}
```

iteration

iteration is similar to index but returns the current iteration number. If you loop three times with the start attribute set to ten, then index will return 10, 11, and 12 respectively; but iteration returns 1, 2, and 3. This is the main difference between index and iteration. iteration has an alias with a similar functionality. This is rownum.

total

This returns the total number of iterations. Note that this is the only variable you can use after the {section} ends.

loop

loop returns the last index number of the loop, which you can use after the loop or inside it.

foreach

{foreach} provides a great facility over {section}. With {foreach} you can iterate through the items of an array and access their properties much more easily as compared to {section}. I personally prefer to use {foreach} all the time. It extracts each item of the array as a separate array containing key-value pairs. You can access each and every property of that extracted object in an associative style. This increases the readability of your code and makes it easy for other team members who work with this code. For example, if you run a query in your database and then fetch the results preserving their keys (that is, using the mysql_fetch_assoc() function) and pass them to Smarty, then the {foreach} loop will extract each row from this whole result set as an associative array. You can access the data of every column for that row in this format: $object.propertyname. This makes your code much more structured and readable. If you want to convert the {section} example shown in the previous section into a {foreach} example, it will look like this:

sample_section2.tpl

```
<table>
{foreach item=book loop=$books}      from
    <tr>
        <td><tmg src={$book.image_id}</td>
        <td>Title: {$book.title}<br/>
            Price: {$book.price}<br/>
            Author: {$book.authors}</td>
    </tr>
{/section}      {/foreach}
```

and the PHP code will be as shown:

sample_section2.php

```
<?
    #...your mysql connection & smarty initialization goes here
    $result = mysql_query(SELECT title, image, price, author from books LIMIT
20);
    while ($row = mysql_fetch_assoc($result)
    {
        $book['title'] = $row['title'];
        $book['image_id'] = $row['image'];
        $book['price'] = $row['images'];
        $book['authors'] = $row['author'];
        $books[] = $book;
    }
    $smarty->assign("books",$books);
    $smarty->display("sample_section2.tpl");

?>
```

Templates in the Real World

Now that we have discussed the basics, let's see how templates work in real-world problems. We will show you how to develop some templates that can solve your everyday problems. These are listed below:

- Calendar
- Generalized Database Reports
- Data Input Forms
- Email Newsletter

Calendar

Calendar is a HTML gadget you may occasionally need for a website. If you plan to develop a calendar, don't worry about writing many lines of code. Using Smarty, you can develop it in a very straightforward way. Let's see how.

calendar.tpl

```
<b>{$title}</b>
{html_table loop=$special_days cols=7}
</body>
</html>
```

In this template, we use a special Smarty function named {html_table}. We will discuss this in detail, later in this section. First let's take a look at the PHP script that assigns the variables to display the calendar.

calendar.php

```
<?
    include("libs/smarty.class.php");
    $smarty = new smarty();

    $date = "10/01/2005"; //October 01, 2005
```

```
        $week_days = array("Sat"=>1, "Sun"=>2, "Mon"=>3,"Tue"=>4,"Wed"=>5,
"Thu"=>6,"Fri"=>7);

        $total_day_of_month = get_total_day($date);
        $starting_day = $week_days[Date("D",strtotime($date))] - 1;
        foreach (array_keys($week_days) as $day)
        $days[] = $day;
        for ($i=0; $i<$starting_day; $i++)
        $days[] = " ";
        for ($i=1; $i< ($total_day_of_month+1); $i++)
        $days[] = $i;

        $smarty->assign("title","October 2005");
        $smarty->assign("special_days", $days);
        $smarty->display("calendar.tpl");

    function get_total_day($date)
    {
        $time_stamp = strtotime($date);
        $month_ar = split("/", $date);
        $month = $month_ar[0];
        $year = Date("Y",$time_stamp);
        for ($i=28; $i<33; $i++)
        {
            if (!checkdate($month, $i, $year)){
                return ($i - 1);
            }
        }
    }
}
?>
```

If you run this script in a browser you will see the following output:

Note that in the code, we supplied the date in the $date variable. If you change it to 11/01/05 then you will see the following output.

That's it, you're done!. Have you noticed how small the template is? As we said, we use a special Smarty function {html_table}. This takes an array as parameter and an optional column number. By default the column number is set to 3. Here we need seven columns for a calendar, so we specified cols=7. Then it displays the array as a table splitting it into specified number of columns in each row.

Database Report

Database reports are the most common examples where Smarty is used. With Smarty, you can develop smashing reports in a minute. However, if you want to your reports to look good, you must have some knowledge about CSS. For this example, we have the following tables:

```
mysql> DESC agents;
+------------+--------------+------+-----+---------+-------+
| Field      | Type         | Null | Key | Default | Extra |
+------------+--------------+------+-----+---------+-------+
| area       | varchar(50)  |      |     |         |       |
| agent_id   | int(11)      |      |     | 0       |       |
| agent_name | varchar(255) |      |     |         |       |
+------------+--------------+------+-----+---------+-------+

mysql> DESC items;
+------------+--------------+------+-----+---------+-------+
| Field      | Type         | Null | Key | Default | Extra |
+------------+--------------+------+-----+---------+-------+
| item_id    | varchar(10)  |      |     |         |       |
| item_name  | varchar(255) |      |     |         |       |
| item_price | int(11)      |      |     | 0       |       |
+------------+--------------+------+-----+---------+-------+
```

```
mysql> DESC sales;
+----------+-------------+------+-----+---------+-------+
| Field    | Type        | Null | Key | Default | Extra |
+----------+-------------+------+-----+---------+-------+
| agent_id | int(11)     |      |     | 0       |       |
| item_id  | varchar(10) |      |     | 0       |       |
| quantity | int(11)     |      |     | 0       |       |
+----------+-------------+------+-----+---------+-------+
3 rows in set (0.00 sec)
```

database_report.php

```php
<?
include("libs/smarty.class.php");
$smarty= new smarty();
mysql_connect("localhost","root","root");
mysql_select_db("smarty");
$result = mysql_query("SELECT area,
                              agent_name,
                              item_name,
                              quantity,
                              item_price,
                              (quantity*item_price) as total
                    FROM    agents
        INNER JOIN sales on agents.agent_id = sales.agent_id
        INNER JOIN items on sales.item_id = items.item_id
        ORDER BY area ASC");
while ($row = mysql_fetch_assoc($result))
{
    $areas[] = $row['area'];
    $agents[] = $row['agent_name'];
    $items[] = $row['item_name'];
    $quantities[] = $row['quantity'];
    $total[] = $row['total'];
}

$fields = array("area", "agent", "item", "quantity", "total");

$smarty->assign("areas", $areas);
$smarty->assign("agents", $agents);
$smarty->assign("items", $items);
$smarty->assign("quantities", $quantities);
$smarty->assign("total", $total);
$smarty->assign("fields", $fields);
$smarty->display("database_report.tpl");
mysql_free_result($result);
?>
```

This script executes a query and fetches the records. It then makes an array of each item and assigns it to a Smarty variable. Now, it's time to develop the template for the report. Let's go.

database_report.tpl

```html
<html>
<body>
<table cellpadding="4" border="1" cellspacing="0"><tr>
{section name=id loop=$fields}
<th>{$fields[id]}</th>
{/section}
</tr>
{section name=data loop=$areas}
<tr>
<td>{$areas[data]}</td>
```

64

```
<td>{$agents[data]}</td>
<td>{$items[data]}</td>
<td>{$quantities[data]}</td>
<td>{$total[data]}</td>
</tr>
{/section}
</table>
</body>
</html>
```

Now run this script and you will get the following output:

You get a basic database report with not much attention paid to its presentation and look. The template code is so simple that Smarty beginners can easily understand it. Let's see how we can make this report look better with another Smarty function, cycle.

cycle is a Smarty function that just cycles through a set of values and returns them one by one. This function is extremely useful when you are trying to choose alternating values for a specific purpose. For an example, if we change the background color of every <tr> element then definitely it will look more pleasant. Let's see the {cycle} function in action. Just replace the <tr> on the ninth line in the above template with the following code:

```
<tr bgcolor='{cycle values="#EBEBEB, #ACABAB"}'>
```

Now run the script and you will see the following output:

Smarty gives you extremely powerful functions for doing everything you would like to.

Let's apply some CSS over your template. We will just change the `<th>` style, and remove the table border and add the following style definition at the beginning of the `database_report.tpl` file.

```
<style>
#report_table th{
    border: 1px solid;
    /*padding-left: 15px;*/
    padding-right: 30px;
    color: #EEEEEC;
    background-color: #25510D;
    text-align: left;
}
#report_table {
    border: 1px solid #cccccc;
}
</style>
```

We will also replace the third line of our previous template code with this one:

```
<table cellpadding="4" border="0" cellspacing="1" id='report_table' ><tr>
```

Now see the output.

Just note that we used a specific table id and CSS only to avoid CSS cross referencing. Always practice this to avoid unexpected results.

Data Input Forms

Data input forms are required in almost all web applications. Smarty provides some helpful functions to better your form design process. These functions output some HTML objects that generally take time to process via PHP or JavaScript. They come handy when you want to retrieve some information and display it in the edit mode.

For example, let's assume your user has entered his or her skill matrix in different checkboxes. Now you have to retrieve this information from the database and show it in the same format as your user entered it initially: that is, some checkboxes remain checked while others remain unchecked. This scenario becomes extremely complex if you want to achieve this using only PHP.

In the following example, we will make a user survey form and show it in edit mode according to your user's given input. We should have a combo box, checkbox and radio buttons in our input form. We will not go through the details of saving this data in a database. Instead we will concentrate on techniques for displaying it in edit mode.

survey.tpl

```
<html>
<head>
<title>Survey Form</title>
<style type="text/css">
{literal}
body,td,th {
    font-family: Verdana, Arial, Helvetica, sans-serif;
    font-size: 12px;
}
{/literal}
</style>
</head>
<body>
<p><strong>Survey Form</strong></p>
<form name="survey_form" method="post" action="">
  <table width="339" border="0" cellpadding="4" cellspacing="0">
    <tr>
      <td width="165">Name: </td>
      <td width="158"><input name="name" type="text" id="name"
          value="{$name}"></td>
    </tr>
    <tr>
      <td>Email: </td>
      <td><input name="email" type="text" id="email" value="{$email}"></td>
    </tr>
    <tr>
      <td>Country: </td>
      <td><select name="country">
        {html_options options=$countries selected=$country}
        </select></td>
    </tr>
    <tr>
      <td>State: </td>
      <td><select name="state">
        {html_options options=$states selected=$state}
                </select></td>
    </tr>
    <tr>
      <td valign="top">Company Name: </td>
      <td><p>
        <input type="text" name="company_name">
        <br>
        {$company_start}</p>          </td>
    </tr>
    <tr>
      <td valign="top">Company Starts: </td>
      <td>{html_select_date}</td>
    </tr>
    <tr>
      <td valign="top">Yearly Revenue of your Company: </td>
      <td>{html_radios name="yearly_revenue" options=$revenues
          selected=$revenue separator="<br />"}
</td>
    </tr>
    <tr>
      <td valign="top">Primary OS: </td>
      <td>
      <p>{html_checkboxes name="os" options=$oses selected=$os
          separator="<br />"}</p>
      </td>
    </tr>
  </table>
</form>
</body>
</html>
```

survey.php

```
<?
include_once("libs/smarty.class.php");
$smarty =new smarty();

$smarty->assign("name", "Junayed Ahnaf");
$smarty->assign("email", "junayed@sampledomain.com");

$countries = array("Bangladesh", "India", "Pakistan", "Nepal", "Maldives",
"Srilanka", "Bhutan");
$country = 0;
$smarty->assign("countries", $countries);
$smarty->assign("country", $country);

$states = array("state1", "state2", "state3", "state4", "state5");
$state = 3;
$smarty->assign("states", $states);
$smarty->assign("state", $state);

$smarty->assign("company_name", "My World");
$smarty->assign("company_start_date", "12/2001");


$smarty->assign('revenues', array(
        1 => '$0-$10000',
        2 => '$10000-$20000',
        3 => '$20000-$50000',
        4 => '$50000+'));
$smarty->assign('revenue', 2);

$smarty->assign('oses', array(
        1 => 'Windows XP',
        2 => 'Linux',
        3 => 'Sun Solaris',
        4 => 'Mac OS'));
$smarty->assign("os", array(2,1));
$smarty->display("survey.tpl");
?>
```

To keep the coding simple, I hard-coded the variable assignments in the above example. In a real-life application, of course, this data would be retrieved from a database or other source.

The first time that the user visits this page, these variables have no value. The visitor will see all those HTML objects with no pre-selected value at all. When the user selects something then we will store it in the database.

The main goal of this example is to show how to retrieve the data items and show them in edit mode while keeping the code simple. Let's see how the form will be displayed in a browser for first time.

In this template we used some special Smarty functions like {html_radios}, {html_checkboxes}, {html_select_date}, and {html_options}. {html_radios} and {html_checkboxes} are used to generate a group of radio buttons and checkboxes. Moreover, you can define the values that will be pre-selected for these functions. This feature makes them usable in real life, because pre-selecting these checkboxes with retrieved information is a big hassle, whether you do it on the server side or client side. Smarty makes it easy for template designers. {html_select_date} returns a set of combo boxes to make it easy to select dates. You can control the range of years and dates. {html_select_date} has a similar sibling that just gives you the facility to select time instead of date; this is {html_select_time}. We will discuss these functions in detail in Chapter 6.

Email Newsletter

Newsletters are a very popular way to broadcast news about the products of a company or whatever. Due to extensive use of email, these days email newsletters are gaining popularity. You can use Smarty to generate attractive newsletters for your users and send them as HTML mail. Here we will show you a fixed design for this, but in practice you would like to pre-design a bunch of templates for your newsletters. In this example, we will generate a newsletter with Smarty and broadcast it using the **MIME** mail sending capability of PHP.

newsletter.tpl

```
<table width="90%"  border="0" align="center" cellspacing="5">
  <tr>
    <td bgcolor="#FFFFFF"><img
      src="http://www.packtpub.com/images/Packt.png"></td>
    <td><div align="right">
      <h3>Newsletter Issue {$issue} {$month}, {$year} </h3>
    </div></td>
  </tr>
  <tr>
    <td width="31%" bgcolor="#999999"><table width="100%"  border="0"
      cellpadding="0" cellspacing="1">
      <tr>
        <td bgcolor="#999999"><div align="center"><strong>Books published in
this week </strong></div></td>
      </tr>
      {section name=book loop=$books}
      <tr>
        <td bgcolor="#FFFFFF"><div align="center"><img src='{$images[book]}'
          vspace="2"><br />
          <b>{$books[book]}</b> </div></td>
      </tr>
      {/section}
    </table></td>
    <td width="69%" valign="top">
    <p>
        <b>{$reviews.title}</b><br/>
        {$reviews.description}<br/>
        Read More : <a href='{$reviews.link}'>Click Here</a>
    </p>      </td>
  </tr>
  <tr>
    <td colspan="2"><div align="center"> &copy; Packt Publishing Ltd 2005
</div></td>
  </tr>
</table>
```

This is an imaginary newsletter for Packt Publishing. Let's assume they plan to distribute it weekly with news of published titles and reviews about their books particular to that week. We will now look at the script to generate a newsletter from this template and send it as an HTML mail to users who subscribed to receive their newsletter. Following is a preview of our newsletter.

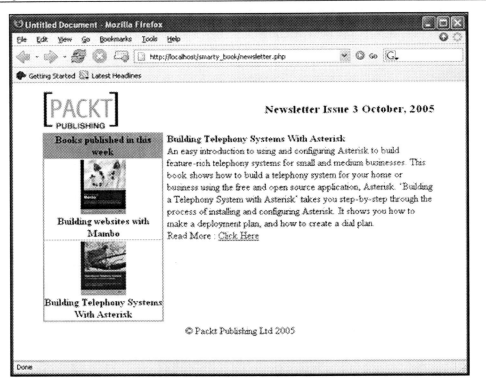

newsletter.php

```php
<?
include ("libs/smarty.class.php");
$smarty = new smarty();

$smarty->assign("issue", 3);
$smarty->assign("month","October");
$smarty->assign("year", 2005);

$books = array("Building websites with Mambo","Building Telephony Systems With
Asterisk");
$images =
array("http://www.packtpub.com/images/73x90/1904811736.png","http://www.packtp
ub.com/images/73x90/1904811159.png");

$smarty->assign("books", $books);
$smarty->assign("images", $images);

$review = <<< END
An easy introduction to using and configuring Asterisk to build feature-rich
telephony systems for small and medium businesses.
This book shows how to build a telephony system for your home or business
using the free and open source application, Asterisk. 'Building a Telephony
System with Asterisk' takes you step-by-step through the process of installing
and configuring Asterisk. It shows you how to make a deployment plan, and how
to create a dial plan.
END;
```

```
$link = "http://www.packtpub.com/asterisk/book";
$title = "Building Telephony Systems With Asterisk";
$reviews = array("title"=>$title,
                 "description"=>$review,
                 "link"=>$link);
$smarty->assign("reviews", $reviews);

$output = $smarty->fetch("newsletter.tpl");

$user = "someuser@somedomain.com";

$headers = "MIME-Version: 1.0 \n" ;
$headers .= "Content-Type: text/html; charset=iso-8859-1 \n";
$headers .= "From: newsletter@my_domain.com \n";

mail($user, "Newsletter", $out, $headers);
?>
```

We used a special Smarty method `fetch()` instead of `display()`. This method renders the template with variables and returns the rendered HTML to a variable. Though we need to send the newsletter, we have to capture the rendered output into a variable for further processing. That's why we used `fetch()`. Then we used PHP's built-in email sending capability to send this newsletter as an HTML mail.

> In the real world you shouldn't send newsletters as HTML mails as many mail service providers do not support HTML mails and mails sent through them will be shown simply as plain text with HTML tags. Therefore, you should always send a plain-text copy to your users. The best practice is to ask users whether they want to receive HTML mails or plain text mails and send newsletters according to their choice.

Running PHP Code Inside your Templates

The main objective of Smarty is to separate the business logic layer from presentation layer. Therefore, a template should never contain business logic and the business logic layer should never contain HTML. Smarty is an extremely powerful templating language and gives you maximum flexibility as compared to other template engines. In Smarty, you can even run PHP code directly inside your template. Though this is not recommended, you may need it in some rare cases.

Smarty has a {php} tag. If you write PHP code inside a {php}{/php} tag block, it will be executed directly. Let's see the following example:

php_code.tpl
```
{php}
echo "This is PHP Code executing directly<br />";
for($i=0; $i<3; $i++)
echo "But it's better to avoid embedding PHP code in your template<br />";
{/php}
```

And here is the script to display it.

php_code.php

```
<?
include("libs/smarty.class.php");
$smarty = new smarty();
$smarty->display("php_code.tpl")
?>
```

If you run the script, you will see the following output. PHP codes are executed as usual.

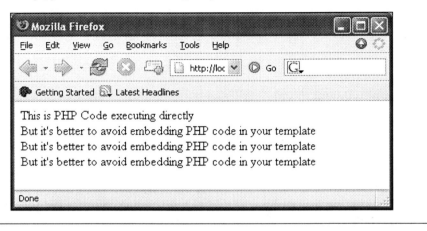

Template programmers, you still you have the key in your hand. If you are worried about security and don't want to allow some specific PHP functions from your templates, you can block them from being used. In the next chapter we will show you how.

Summary

We have gone through the details of designing templates in this chapter and I am sure that you are already impressed with Smarty. We have seen how templates can solve your daily needs in web development and how you can start designing cool templates. If you use Smarty regularly, you will find many more easy techniques to solve complex design problems. Smarty gives you the ultimate power for designing and programming templates. In the next chapter, we will go into the details of process control, configuration files for temporary storage, and variable modifiers, which will ease the processing of variables to a great extent.

5
Advanced Templating

In the previous chapter, you have learned about the basic workflow of Smarty templates. We demonstrated how you can implement conditions and loops, and also demonstrated usage of some necessary Smarty functions that are used in everyday web applications. However, there are a lot of features that you are not familiar with as yet. In this chapter we will give you a basic introduction to plug-ins and modifiers. We will also go through the creation of two advanced web applications, which will further clear your concepts. By the end of this chapter you will be introduced to configuration files, a special storage medium for storing the value of Smarty variables and using them later.

Smarty under the Hood

This section will clear any doubts you may have regarding the actual working of Smarty templates. Whenever the Smarty engine is called to render a template file, it compiles the template into native PHP code for the first time. Let's dissect a compiled template and take a detailed look at the template itself.

profiles.tpl

```
<body>
{foreach item=student from=$students}
<table width="80%" border="1" cellspacing="0" cellpadding="4">
  <tr>
    <td width="38%" bgcolor="#CCCCCC" ><strong>Profile of
{$student.nick}</strong></td>
    <td width="62%"> </td>
  </tr>
  <tr>
    <td>Name : </td>
    <td>{$student.name}</td>
  </tr>
  <tr>
    <td>Born</td>
    <td>{$student.born}</td>
  </tr>
  <tr>
    <td>Blood Group </td>
    <td>{$student.blood_grp}</td>
  </tr>
  <tr>
    <td>Email</td>
```

```
        <td>{$student.email}</td>
    </tr>
</table><br/>
{/foreach}
</body>
```

In this template, we look through profiles of some students. Now take a look at the compiled version of this template.

%%EB^EB9^EB93DE89%%profiles.tpl.php

```
<?php /* Smarty version 2.6.7, created on 2005-09-27 08:14:22
        compiled from profiles.tpl */ ?>
<body>
<?php if (count($_from = (array)$this->_tpl_vars['students'])):
    foreach ($_from as $this->_tpl_vars['student']):
?>
<table width="80%"  border="1" cellspacing="0" cellpadding="4">
  <tr>
    <td width="38%" bgcolor="#CCCCCC" ><strong>Profile of <?php echo
$this->_tpl_vars['student']['nick']; ?>
</strong></td>
        <td width="62%"> </td>
    </tr>
    <tr>
      <td>Name : </td>
      <td><?php echo $this->_tpl_vars['student']['name']; ?>
</td>
    </tr>
    <tr>
      <td>Born</td>
      <td><?php echo $this->_tpl_vars['student']['born']; ?>
</td>
    </tr>
    <tr>
      <td>Blood Group </td>
      <td><?php echo $this->_tpl_vars['student']['blood_grp']; ?>
</td>
    </tr>
    <tr>
      <td>Email</td>
      <td><?php echo $this->_tpl_vars['student']['email']; ?>
</td>
    </tr>
</table><br/>
<?php endforeach; endif; unset($_from); ?>
</body>
```

This is pure PHP code, isn't it? The first two lines of this compiled template are simply a timestamp created by Smarty, which describes the version of the Smarty engine used to compile this template. The date of compilation is also indicated.

The third and fourth lines are PHP code that determines if anything is supplied to Smarty itself as an array in the students variable. If anything is found, it will extract each element of that array in the $_from variable and proceed through the loop. Again each element of this $_from is accessed via the $this->_tpl_vars['student'] variable. All variables passed to the Smarty engine by PHP script are stored in a global _tpl_vars[] array. This _tpl_vars[] is an internal global variable of the Smarty engine. Now you understand that compiled templates are nothing but pure PHP code. Hence they run much faster. Whenever a PHP script asks Smarty to compile a template, it first looks in the compiled templates directory and checks if a compiled version is available or not. If

Smarty finds a compiled version of that template, it will not bother to compile it again unless the original template code has been modified. For these internal processes Smarty is comparatively faster than many other template engines.

Compile Steps

Lets discuss the steps by which a Smarty template is compiled:

1. Smarty applies prefilters (if any) over the whole template.
2. All built-in functions and tags are processed.
3. All custom modifiers are processed.
4. All custom block functions are processed. In this case if nested blocks are found then the *deepest* block is processed first, then its parent is processed and so forth until all the blocks are processed successfully.
5. Smarty applies postfilters (if any).
6. We get the compiled templates.

Prefilters and Postfilters

Prefilters are functions that are applied on your template before it is compiled. They are very useful if you want to do some cleanup or preformatting before the compilation starts. You can even use them for cleaning up the comments to reduce the output size. Postfilters are applied after your template is compiled. However, filters are rarely used in real-life applications. Most developers usually use modifiers and functions.

What is a Smarty Modifier?

Smarty modifiers are custom functions that process the value of any variable to achieve something special that is not available otherwise. For example, if you wish to capitalize the variable, concatenate some variables, or to perform string replace operations, then modifiers are the best way to do it. You can apply modifiers to variables and custom functions. You can also pass parameters to variable modifiers. Modifiers are a special kind of Smarty plug-in.

Stretch your Imagination with Smarty

In this section we will go through some wild and complex Smarty examples that are guaranteed to stretch your imagination. We will see a complex student transcript template and a photo gallery. The main goal of this section is to introduce you to advanced templating and to teach you how to manipulate very complex nested arrays structures.

Student Transcript

A student transcript is the most common example for Smarty template designers. In this, all the course results are supplied as a big nested array and you have to process them all and finally show a printable transcript.

We will use a dummy transcript model here with some dummy subjects. For this, assume we get a very complex array structure like this:

```
Array
(
    [Fall 2005] => Array
        (
            [math-I] => Array
                (
                    [title] => Prelimenary Mathematics
                    [grade] => A+
                )

            [eng-I] => Array
                (
                    [title] => Basic English
                    [grade] => A+
                )

        )

    [Spring 2006] => Array
        (
            [math-II] => Array
                (
                    [title] => Basic Calculus
                    [grade] => A+
                )

            [ch-II] => Array
                (
                    [title] => Advanced Chemistry
                    [grade] => B+
                )

        )

)
```

Let's see how to process these deeply nested arrays and make them printable. Firstly, here are the table structures:

Table Name: Grade

Field	Type	Null	Key	Default	Extra
id	varchar(20)				
course_id	varchar(30)				
semester_id	varchar(30)				
grade	varchar(5)				

Table Name: Courses

Field	Type	Null	Key	Default	Extra
course_id	varchar(30)				
course_title	varchar(255)				
course_credit	float			0	

transcript.tpl

```
<body>
{literal}
<style>
.border_bottom
{
    border-bottom: 1px solid;
}
</style>
{/literal}
<h2>Transcript of {$roll}</h2>
<h4>Total Credit Completed : {$total}</h4>
<hr noshade />
<table width="791" align="center">
{foreach key=semester item=subjects from=$data}
  <tr>
    <td width="134" class="border_bottom"><strong>semester:</strong></td>
    <td width="248" class="border_bottom"><strong>{$semester}</strong></td>
    <td width="126" class="border_bottom"> </td>
    <td width="61" class="border_bottom"> </td>
    <td width="61" class="border_bottom"> </td>
  </tr>
  {foreach key=course_code item=data from=$subjects name=subject}
    <tr>
    <td> {$smarty.foreach.subject.iteration}</td>
    <td> {$course_code}</td>
    <td> {$data.title}</td>
    <td> {$data.credit}</td>
    <td> {$data.grade}</td>
    </tr>
  {/foreach}
  {/foreach}

</table>
</body>
```

transcript.php

```php
<?
mysql_connect("localhost", "root", "root");
mysql_select_db("smarty");
$result = mysql_query("select  semester_id,  courses.course_id, course_title,
course_credit, grade from grade, courses where id='97016' and
courses.course_id = grade.course_id");
while ($row = mysql_fetch_assoc($result))
{
    $semester[$row['semester_id']][$row['course_id']]=array("title"=>$row['cou
rse_title'], "grade"=>$row['grade'], "credit"=>$row['course_credit']);
    $total_credit += $row['course_credit'];
}

include("libs/smarty.class.php");
$smarty = new smarty();
$smarty->assign("data", $semester);
$smarty->assign("roll","97016");
$smarty->assign("total",$total_credit);
$smarty->display("transcript.tpl");
?>
```

The output is as follows:

Transcript of 97016

Total Credit Completed : 29

semester:	Fall 2005			
1	math-I	Prelimenary Mathematics	4	A+
2	eng-I	Basic English	4	A+
3	eng-II	Advanced English	4	A
4	ph-I	Fundamental Physics	3	B+
5	ch-I	Fundamental Chemistry	3	A+
semester:	Spring 2006			
1	math-II	Basic Calculus	3	A+
2	ph-II	Advanced Physics	4	A
3	ch-II	Advanced Chemistry	4	B+

Photo Gallery

A photo gallery is another application that you may need in your everyday web applications. Smarty can help you to design fantastic templates for your photo gallery. Here, we will see the template for a gallery page.

gallery.php

```
<?
include("libs/smarty.class.PHP");
$smarty = new smarty();
define("FILE_PER_PAGE",10);
$offset=$_REQUEST['file_id'];
$page=$_REQUEST['page'];

$offset = (int) $offset;
$page = (int) $page;
$start_offset = $page*FILE_PER_PAGE;

$fp = opendir("images");
while(false !== ($file = readdir($fp)))
{
    if ($file != "." && $file != "..")
    {
        $files[] = $file;
    }
}
$total_pages = ceil(count($files)/FILE_PER_PAGE);
for ($i=0; $i<$total_pages; $i++)
$pages[] = $i+1;


for ($i=$start_offset; $i<$start_offset+FILE_PER_PAGE; $i++)
{
    $temp_offset = $i-$start_offset;
    $temp_linked_files[] = "<a
```

```
href='gallery.php?file_id={$temp_offset}&page={$page}'><img
src='images/{$files[$i]}' height=75 width=100></a>";
    $temp_files[] = $files[$i];
}


$current_file = $temp_files[$offset];


$smarty->assign("pages", $pages);
$smarty->assign("current_file", $current_file);
$smarty->assign("files", $temp_files);
$smarty->assign("linked_files", $temp_linked_files);

$smarty->display("gallery.tpl");
?>
```

gallery.tpl

```
<html>
<head>
<title>Photo Gallery</title>
<meta http-equiv="Content-Type" content="text/html; charset=iso-8859-1">
</head>
{literal}
<script>
function initialize()
{
  var file_id = document.getElementById("file_id");
  file_id.value=0;

}
</script>
{/literal}

<body>
<form name="form1" method="post" action="">
  <table width="100%">
    <tr>
      <td width="47%"><h1>Photo Gallery </h1></td>
       <input name="file_id" type="hidden" id="file_id">
      <td width="53%" align="right"> Page :
<select name=page>

    {html_options options=$pages}
</select>

        <input type="submit" name="Submit" value="Go"
onfocus="initialize();"></td>
      </tr>
    </table>
</form>
<hr size="0">
<table width="100%">
  <tr>
```

```
    <td width="47%" valign="top">{html_table loop=$linked_files}
</td>
    <td width="53%" align="right"><img width="403" height="283" border="1"
src="images/{$current_file}"></td>
  </tr>
</table>
<p> </p>
</body>
</html>
```

The output is as follows:

In the above .tpl file, we used an external thumbnail generator thumb.php. This is a very basic photo gallery, which you can extend easily according to your choice. We here assumed that all images are placed in a folder images in the same directory as this script.

Available Modifiers

As mentioned before, modifiers are nothing but custom PHP functions that work in conjunction with Smarty. In this section we will go through Smarty modifiers and show an example for each of them to help you to master them.

capitalize

capitalize makes the first character of every word capital. It processes the entire variable. PHP has a similar function called ucwords(). The capitalize modifier takes one optional parameter, which determines whether to capitalize words containing numbers or not. If this parameter is true, for example apollo13 will not become Apollo13. By default, this parameter is set to false.

capitalize.tpl

```
<body>
Before using modifier: {$somevalue}
After  using modifier: {$somevalue|capitalize}
</body>
```

capitalize.php

```
<?
include("libs/smarty.class.PHP");
$smarty = new smarty();
$smarty->assign("somevalue","bangladesh is a small country in south asia");
$smarty->display("capitalize.tpl");
?>
```

Output

Before using modifier: Bangladesh is a small country in south asia
After using modifier: Bangladesh Is A Small Country In South Asia

count_characters

Smarty gives you the facility to count the number of characters present in a variable. You can use the count_characters modifier for this purpose. This modifier also takes one optional parameter (by default set to false), which determines whether to count white spaces as characters or not.

count_characters.tpl

```
<body>
Total number of characters in '{$somevalue}' is {$somevalue|count_characters}.
If you consider white spaces, then it is {$somevalue|count_characters:true}
</body>
```

count_characters.php

```
<?
include("libs/smarty.class.php");
$smarty = new smarty();
$smarty->assign("somevalue","bangladesh is a small country in south asia");
$smarty->display("count_characters.tpl");
?>
```

Output

Total number of characters in 'bangladesh is a small country in south asia' is 36. If you consider white space, then it is 43

cat

`cat` is a concatenating modifier for Smarty, which joins two string values together. It takes one optional parameter, which is the string value to be appended to the variable this modifier is used with.

cat.tpl

```
<body>
Kader {$somevalue|cat:"but he didn't like it"}
</body>
```

cat.php

```
<?
include("libs/smarty.class.php");
$smarty = new smarty();
$smarty->assign("somevalue","bought a shirt yesterday");
$smarty->display("cat.tpl");
?>
```

Output

Kader bought a shirt yesterday but he didn't like it

count_paragraphs

This modifier is similar to `count_characters` except that it counts the number of paragraphs in a given string. This modifier takes no parameter.

count_paragraphs.tpl

```
<body>
The total number of paragraphs in the supplied text is
{$somevalue|count_paragraphs}
</body>
```

count_paragraphs.php

```
<?
include("libs/smarty.class.php");
$smarty = new smarty();
$paragraphs = <<< EOD
This is paragraph 1
This is paragraph 2
This is paragraph 3
EOD;

$smarty->assign("somevalue",$paragraphs);
$smarty->display("count_paragraphs.tpl");?>
```

Output

The total number of paragraphs in the supplied text is 3

count_sentences

This modifier counts the number of sentences in the supplied variable. This also takes no parameter. This modifier is helpful when you want to show an excerpt from a big text paragraph (an article or story) by truncating when the number of sentences is more than a predefined value.

count_words

This is another modifier in same group as above. It counts the number of words available in a supplied text in a variable. This takes no parameter at all.

count_words.tpl

```
<body>
The total number of words in the supplied text is {$somevalue|count_words}
</body>
```

count_words.php

```
<?
include("libs/smarty.class.php");
$smarty = new smarty();
$words = "smarty is a leading template engine for PHP developers. It is easy
to use and extremely flexible to manage. Its learning curve is so short.";

$smarty->assign("somevalue",$words);
$smarty->display("count_words.tpl");?>
```

Output

The total number of words in the supplied text is 25

date_format

The date_format modifier is used to format the date and time according to available predefined formats. You can harness the maximum power of the native PHP date and time format function with this modifier. Usually programmers supply the date and time as a UNIX timestamp (using the strtotime() or mktime() PHP function) and then template designers apply these formats as they want. This modifier takes two optional parameters: one is the date and time format string and the other is an optional date to override the date in the variable itself. The available date and time formats are shown here, taken as is from the Smarty manual:

Format	Result
%a	Abbreviated weekday name according to the current locale
%A	Full weekday name according to the current locale
%b	Abbreviated month name according to the current locale
%B	Full month name according to the current locale
%c	Preferred date and time representation for the current locale
%C	Century number (the year divided by 100 and truncated to an integer, range 00 to 99)

Format	Result
%d	Day of the month as a decimal number (range 00 to 31)
%D	Same as %m/%d/%y
%e	Day of the month as a decimal number; a single digit is preceded by a space (range 1 to 31)
%g	Week-based year within century [00,99]
%G	Week-based year, including the century [0000,9999]
%h	Same as %b
%H	Hour as a decimal number using a 24-hour clock (range 00 to 23)
%I	Hour as a decimal number using a 12-hour clock (range 01 to 12)
%j	Day of the year as a decimal number (range 001 to 366)
%k	Hour (24-hour clock); single digits are preceded by a blank (range 0 to 23)
%l	Hour as a decimal number using a 12-hour clock; single digits preceded by a space (range 1 to 12)
%m	Month as a decimal number (range 01 to 12)
%M	Minute as a decimal number
%n	Newline character
%p	Either 'am' or 'pm' according to the given time value, or the corresponding strings for the current locale
%r	Time in a.m. and p.m. notation
%R	Time in 24 hour notation
%S	Second as a decimal number
%t	Tab character
%T	Current time, equal to %H:%M:%S
%u	Weekday as a decimal number [1,7], with 1 representing Monday
%U	Seek number of the current year as a decimal number, starting with the first Sunday as the first day of the first week
%V	The ISO 8601:1988 week number of the current year as a decimal number, range 01 to 53, where week 1 is the first week that has at least 4 days in the current year, and with Monday as the first day of the week.
%w	Day of the week as a decimal, Sunday being 0
%W	Week number of the current year as a decimal number, starting with the first Monday as the first day of the first week
%x	Preferred date representation for the current locale without the time
%X	Preferred time representation for the current locale without the date
%y	Year as a decimal number without a century (range 00 to 99)
%Y	Year as a decimal number including the century
%Z	Time zone or name or abbreviation

date_format.tpl

```
I was born on {$born|date_format:"%dth %b, %Y"}. It was a sunny
{$born|date_format:"%A"|lower}
```

date_format.php

```
<?
include("libs/smarty.class.PHP");
$smarty = new smarty();
$born = strtotime("08/28/1979");
$smarty->assign("born", $born);
$smarty->display("date_format.tpl");
?>
```

Output

I was born on 28th Aug, 1979. It was a sunny tuesday

default

default is an important modifier for template developers. It will help you publish the default value supplied to it and indirectly check whether it contains something or not. This modifier takes one parameter that will be considered as the *default* value. You may find this function handy to set the title of each of your web pages.

default.tpl

```
<title>{$title|default:"Building websites with smarty"}</title>
<body>
An Example of {$title|default:"Building websites with smarty"}
</body>
```

default.php

```
<?
include("libs/smarty.class.php");
$smarty = new smarty();
$smarty->display("default.tpl");
?>
```

Output

```
<title>Building websites with smarty</title>
<body>
An Example of Building websites with smarty
</body>
```

escape

escape is a Smarty modifier used to escape strings. It has some similar functionality to some of PHP's built-in escaping functionality, but you can use this function in a broader scope. Using this function you can escape a string in following modes:

- HTML escape: escapes HTML entities
- URL escape: URL encodes strings
- Java script escape
- Single quote escape: escapes single quotes
- Hexadecimal escape: escapes strings in hexadecimal mode

Let's look at an example.

escape.tpl

```
1. URL escaped: {$somevalue|escape:"url"}"<br />
1. Hex escaped: {$somevalue|escape:"hex"}"<br />
1. Single Quote escaped: {$somevalue|escape:"quotes"}"<br />
1. HTML escaped: {$somehtml|escape:"html"}"<br />
1. Javascript escaped: {$somescript|escape:"url"}"<br />
```

escape.php

```
<?
include("libs/smarty.class.PHP");
$smarty = new smarty();
$smarty->assign("somevalue", "this is peter's hen");
$smarty->assign("somehtml","<b>This is some bold text </b>");
$smarty->assign("somescript","<script>alert('hello, its
javascript');</script>");
$smarty->display("escape.tpl");
?>
```

Output

```
1. URL escaped: this%20is%20peter%27s%20hen"<br />
1. Hex escaped:
%74%68%69%73%20%69%73%20%70%65%74%65%72%27%73%20%68%65%6e"<br />
1. Single Quote escaped: this is peter\'s hen"<br />
1. HTML escaped: &lt;b&gt;This is some bold text &lt;/b&gt;"<br />
1. Javascript escaped:
%3Cscript%3Ealert%28%27hello%2C%20its%20javascript%27%29%3B%3C%2Fscript%3E"<
br />
```

indent

indent is a Smarty modifier used to format text. As the name suggests, it indents a block of text by a given number of characters. This modifier takes two optional parameters. The first parameter defines how many characters the block has to be indented by and second one specifies the character with which to indent it. By default the second parameter is a white space. This modifier comes in handy when you are developing pages with different text formatting.

indent.tpl

```
This is a sample line<br />
{$sometext|indent:10:"#"}
```

indent.php

```
<?
include("libs/smarty.class.PHP");
$smarty = new smarty();
$smarty->assign("sometext","This is some text to indent");
$smarty->display("indent.tpl");
?>
```

Output

This is a sample line
##########This is some text to indent

lower

The lower modifier makes every character in a given string lower case. It takes no parameter at all. It works in the same way as the lcase() function of PHP.

upper

The upper modifier works in just the opposite way to lower. It makes the characters of a given variable on which the modifier is applied uppercase.

upper_lower.tpl

```
Example of upper: {$lowertext|upper}<br />
Example of lower: {$uppertext|lower}
```

upper_lower.php

```
<?
include("libs/smarty.class.php");
$smarty = new smarty();
$smarty->assign("uppertext","THESE WERE UPPERCASE");
$smarty->assign("lowertext","these were lowercase");
$smarty->display("upper_lower.tpl");
?>
```

Output

Example of upper: THESE WERE LOWERCASE
Example of lower: these were uppercase

nl2br

nl2br stands for new line to break. This modifier converts all new line characters to <br />. This function works in the same way as the nl2br() function in PHP. This function is also extremely helpful in different text formatting scenarios.

nl2br.tpl

```
Following is an example of nl2br</br>
{$sometext|nl2br}
```

nl2br.php

```
<?
include("libs/smarty.class.php");
$smarty = new smarty();
$mytext = <<< EOD
This is a single line with line break
But linebreaks are not visible in HTML.
They need to be replaced with a &lt;br&gt; tag.
EOD;
$smarty->assign("sometext",$mytext);
$smarty->display("nl2br.tpl");
?>
```

Output

Following is an example of nl2br
This is a single line with line break
But linebreaks are not visible in HTML.
They need to be replaced with a <br> tag.

regex_replace

regex_replace is an extremely useful and advanced Smarty modifier for experienced template designers. Though PHP has very good support for regular expressions, Smarty developers also included this one in Smarty. PHP supports two major styles of regex, one is *POSIX Extended*-compatible regular expressions, and the other is *Perl-Compatible regular expressions* or *PCRE*. PCRE is the more familiar style in PHP. It's faster than the POSIX Extended one. The Smarty regex_replace modifier supports the PCRE style.

Regular expressions are beyond the scope of this book. For the sake of simplicity, we are just covering how this specific modifier works.

regex_replace.tpl

```
{$email|regex_replace:"~[a-zA-Z0-9._%-]+@[a-zA-Z0-9._%-]+\.[A-Za-z]+~":"not
visible"}
```

regex_replace.php

```
<?
include("libs/smarty.class.php");
$smarty = new smarty();
$smarty->assign("email","My email address is hasin@somewherein.net");
$smarty->display("regex_replace.tpl");
?>
```

Output

My email address is not visible

replace

replace is a normal modifier, which replaces some text with another portion of text. This modifier works with plain text, not regular expressions.

replace.tpl

```
{$somevalue|replace:"mice":"dogs"}
```

replace.php

```
<?
include("libs/smarty.class.php");
$smarty = new smarty();
$smarty->assign("somevalue", "It's raining cats & mice");
$smarty->display("replace.tpl");
?>
```

Output

It's raining cats & dogs

spacify

spacify is a funny modifier available, which is of no practical use in English. This modifier used to spacify, as it's name explains, some text with a given text. That means it inserts your given text (as parameter) between every character. It takes only one parameter, which is by default, white space.

spacify.tpl

```
{$somevalue|spacify}
```

spacify.php

```
<?
include("libs/smarty.class.php");
$smarty = new smarty();
$smarty->assign("somevalue", "It's raining cats & dogs");
$smarty->display("spacify.tpl");
?>
```

Output

I t ' s r a i n i n g c a t s & d o g s

string_format

The string_format modifier is used to format a string by using predefined string formats. You can format a number into a money format, set its decimal places and so forth. For formatting, you can use all the available formats of PHP's built-in sprintf() function with this modifier. Following are the formats taken as is from PHP manual.

Format	Result
%	A literal percent character. No argument is required.
b	The argument is treated as an integer, and presented as a binary number.
c	The argument is treated as an integer, and presented as the character with that ASCII value.
d	The argument is treated as an integer, and presented as a (signed) decimal number.
e	The argument is treated as scientific notation (e.g. 1.2e+2).
u	The argument is treated as an integer, and presented as an unsigned decimal number.
f	The argument is treated as a float, and presented as a floating-point number (locale aware).
F	The argument is treated as a float, and presented as a floating-point number (non-locale aware). Available since PHP 4.3.10 and PHP 5.0.3.
o	The argument is treated as an integer, and presented as an octal number.
s	The argument is treated as and presented as a string.
x	The argument is treated as an integer and presented as a hexadecimal number (with lowercase letters).
X	The argument is treated as an integer and presented as a hexadecimal number (with uppercase letters).

string_format.tpl

```
The book costs BDT{$somevalue|string_format:"%.2f"}
```

string_format.php

```
<?
include("libs/smarty.class.php");
$smarty = new smarty();
$smarty->assign("somevalue", "1200");
$smarty->display("string_format.tpl");
?>
```

Output

The book costs BDT1200.00

strip

strip is a necessary modifier for Smarty template designers. You can replace tabs, line breaks, and white spaces with a single white space with the help of this modifier. This modifier takes one parameter which is by default white space. This parameter indicates what will be the replacement for the tabs, line breaks, and white spaces in the string on which this modifier is being applied.

strip_tags

The `strip_tags` modifier strips HTML tags from a given string. This modifier takes an optional Boolean parameter by which you can specify which one will be used to replace the tags, white space or nothing. By default this parameter is true, meaning tags are replaced with a white space.

strip_tags.tpl

```
{$sometext|strip_tags}
```

strip_tags.php

```
<?
include("libs/smarty.class.php");
$smarty->assign("sometext", "This is some <b>Bold</b> text");
$smarty->display("strip_tags.tpl");
?>
```

Output

This is some Bold text

truncate

The `truncate` modifier truncates a string at the given point. You can specify after how many characters you will truncate it. This modifier is extremely helpful for article management websites where only truncated excerpts of articles are needed to be shown in the front page. This modifier takes three optional parameters. The first parameter is the number of characters after which the truncation occurs. The second parameter is what will replace the truncated part of the string; by default it is an ellipsis. The third parameter indicates whether the truncate modifier should truncate in the middle of a word of not. If you set the third parameter as false, then it will not truncate in the middle of a word but at the start of it.

truncate.tpl

```
{$sometext|truncate:18:"...":true}<br />
{$sometext|truncate:18:"...":false}
```

truncate.php

```
<?
include("libs/smarty.class.php");
$smarty = new smarty();
$smarty->assign("sometext", "This is some long text to truncate");
$smarty->display("truncate.tpl");
?>
```

Output

This is some lo...

This is some...

Note that when the third parameter is true, it truncates in the middle of a word in the example.

wordwrap

The wordwrap modifier simply wraps up text with a given parameter. This modifier takes three optional parameters. The first parameter specifies after how many character to wrap; by default it is 80. The second parameter is the character to use as a wrapper. And the third parameter works in the same manner as the third parameter of the truncate modifier: it determines whether to break a word or not. In the following example, we added an additional nl2br so that the effect becomes clear to you. As we are using default wrapper, the wordwrap modifier wraps with \n (linebreak or newline character). The nl2br modifier converts these newline characters into <br/>, so the wrap becomes visible to you.

wordwrap.tpl

```
{$sometext|wordwrap:60|nl2br}
```

wordwrap.php

```
<?
include("libs/smarty.class.php");
$smarty = new smarty();
$sometext = <<< EOD
The wordwrap modifier simply wraps up text with a given parameters. This modifier
takes three optional parameters. The first parameter is after how many character
to wrap, by default it is 80. The second optional parameter is the character to
use as wrapper. And the third parameter works in the same manner as the third
parameter of the truncate modifier, it determines whether to break inside a word
of not.
EOD;
$smarty->assign("sometext",$sometext);
$smarty->display("wordwrap.tpl");
?>
```

Output

The wordwrap modifier simply wraps up text with a given

parameter. This modifier takes three optional parameters.

The first parameter is after how many character to wrap, by

default it is 80. The second optional parameter is the

character to use as wrapper. And the third parameter works

in the same manner as the third parameter of the truncate modifier,

it determines whether to break inside a word of not.

Combining Modifiers

Whenever you use modifiers in your template, you can use them singly or you can combine two modifiers and use them. Combining modifiers gives you more power over using them. Combining them is easy; just add them with a pipe | sign one by one.

Let's take a look at the following example. Here we use two modifiers in combination.

date_format.tpl

```
I was born in {$born|date_format:"%dth %b, %Y"}. It was a sunny
{$born|date_format:"%A"|lower}
```

date_format.php

```
<?
include("libs/smarty.class.php");
$smarty = new smarty();
$born = strtotime("08/28/1979");
$smarty->assign("born", $born);
$smarty->display("date_format.tpl");
?>
```

Output

I was born in 28th Aug, 1979. It was a sunny tuesday

Here the Date_format modifier returns the full day name with its first character in upper case, so we used lower modifier in combination with date_format to make it lowercase:
{$born|date_format:"%A"|lower}

That's it. There's no limit on how many modifiers you can combine together. If you can properly use modifiers in combination, it opens the door of power to you, in many cases.

Configuration Files

Configuration files are special files to store the values of variables that could be used later by Smarty template designers. The values you store here are treated as global variables. You must store site configuration information that is needed by many templates in your site in the configuration files. For example, you can store the site title, site footer info, and copyright information in the configuration files. If you hardcode them in your template files and later need to change them then you have to modify all of them; but this information could change often. So if you store them in configuration files and in the template you use these configuration instead of hard coding, that will be much more reusable. Let's look at the format of a configuration file.

Configuration files can store values under sections or without sections. Let's look at the following configuration files:

```
Title = "My Sample Site"
BannerText = "Rock Yourself"
BannerBackground = #104A7B

[NavigationPanel]
THColor = #e3cb8e

[Footer]
CopyrightText = "All rights reserved by Mr X";
```

If you look at the configuration file, you will see it contains one section named [NavigationPanel], another named [Footer], and three global variables.

Now the question comes: How do we use this configuration file in practice? Smarty gives template designers a function for this purpose. It is {config_load}.

In every template, you can use these three global variables in following way:

sometemplate.tpl
```
{config_load file=myconfiguration.cfg}
<title> {#Title#} </title>
```

That's it!, you can use any variable from the configuration file as {#VariableName#} after loading the configuration file.

Let's see how you can use variables under a section.

footer.tpl
```
{config_load file=myconfiguration.cfg section= "Footer"}
<title> {#CopyrightText#} </title>
```

See how useful these configuration files could be. We will not go further with configuration files in this chapter. They will come again in later chapters, in detail.

Summary

So you have an understanding on some advanced topics like deeply nested arrays and variable modifiers, which give you the ultimate power over template designing. If you use your imagination properly and utilize these modifiers, Smarty will prove to be the ultimate tool for you. Also in real life you will get very complex array structures, but manipulating them will depend on practice. All you have to do is maintain proper communication with the programmers who supply the data. In the next chapters you will get a clear idea about Smarty functions. Happy Smartying!

6
Smarty Functions

Smarty provides a wide variety of functions available to you as a template designer to use as part of your templates. While you may never use some of these functions, it is important to get to know their functionality, as they were created with the ultimate goal of solving everyday problems of web developers.

As a rule of thumb, if you need some functionality in your templates and you don't know for sure if Smarty already provides it, check if there is already a function for it. If you require some custom functionality, consider writing a Smarty plug-in.

In this chapter you will learn about the different types of functions available in Smarty, a list of those functions and examples of their use, and how to extend Smarty and create your own functions.

Types of Smarty Functions

Smarty as a software project tries to be simple and this is seen in the built-in functionality that is shipped by the template compiler and parser. The template language is itself built on functions that enable the basis of the functionality of a template, and you can extend the standard functionality of Smarty with plug-ins. However, the built-in functions cannot be modified and you cannot create custom functions with the same names.

Since the development team knew that they couldn't predict all uses of Smarty, or all needed functions, they decided to create a plug-in architecture and let the end users create, modify, and submit new plug-ins. Most of the Smarty functions are themselves implemented using this very plug-in architecture.

Functions in Action

We will build a relatively complex site in this chapter, while explaining step by step the strengths and weaknesses of particular functions. At the end of this chapter, you should be able to choose the appropriate functions when you need some help from Smarty.

Let's start this process with a simple web page, a front page for a company website, along with its template.

index.tpl

```
<html>
<head>
<title>Smarty LLC</title>
</head>
<body>
<h3>Smarty LLC</h3>
<p>We provide consulting services to the healthcare industry.</p>
<p>For more details, please contact us by email on contact@smartyllc.com</p>
</body>
</html>
```

index.php

```
<?php
include_once('libs/Smarty.class.php');
$smarty = new Smarty;
$smarty->display('index.tpl');
?>
```

This is a simple website, with just one page. Let's expand this by creating a couple of different pages, one listing the management team of our company, and another displaying a separate screen with a contact form instead of telling potential customers to send an email to a particular address.

Here's the page listing the management team:

about.tpl

```
<html>
<head>
 <title>Smarty LLC</title>
</head>
<body>

<h3>Smarty LLC: Management Team</h3>

<p><b>Julian Fox, CEO</b> - Julian handles all management issues related to
the company, such as dealing with potential customers and providing a clear
strategy for services.</p>

<p><b>Ryan Foster, CTO</b> - Ryan handles all technical aspects of consulting
services available through Smarty LLC.</p>

</body>
</html>
```

And the following will be the new contact page. We will not provide the PHP code to actually send out emails from the contact form, but that's simple and can be looked up on the Internet.

contact.tpl

```
<html>
<head>
 <title>Smarty LLC</title>
</head>
<body>

<h3>Smarty LLC: Contact Us</h3>
```

```
<form method="post" action="contact_us.php">
<p>
 <b>Your Name:</b><br />
 <input type="text" name="name" size="40">
</p>

<p>
 <b>Your Email:</b><br />
 <input type="text" name="email" size="40">
</p>

<p>
 <b>Your Message:</b><br />
 <textarea name="message" cols="40" rows="10"></textarea>
</p>

<input type="submit" value="Send Message">
</form>

</body>
</html>
```

So now we have a slightly more complicated website, and some challenges are starting to appear. Even though our collection of pages is still small, every change in a section of the site that is used by all of these pages will require three different changes. Let's use some of Smarty features to help us with this maintenance headache.

Action: Re-using Page Elements with the include Function

1. Create the following file and save it as header.tpl in your template directory:

```
<html>
<head>
 <title>Smarty LLC</title>
</head>
<body>
```

2. Create another file called footer.tpl in the same location, with the following content:

```
</body>
</html>
```

3. Now make the following changes to your existing web pages:

   - Replace the following HTML snippets:

   ```
   <html>
   <head>
   <title>Smarty LLC</title>
   </head>
   <body>
   ```

   With:

   ```
   {include file="header.tpl"}
   ```

   - Substitute the following:

   ```
   </body>
   </html>
   ```

   With:

   ```
   {include file="footer.tpl"}
   ```

4. Open your web browser and take a look at your website again. You should see exactly what you were seeing before. Try adding an image tag to add the image `new.jpg` to your `header.tpl` template file, and reloading the website in your browser. You should see the new image on all the web pages, as shown:

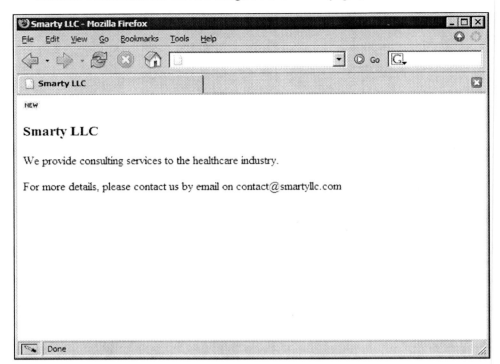

Explanation

The interesting thing about the `include()` function is that it is a pretty powerful way of modularizing your templates, and easing the maintenance work that you must do in the future. Instead of changing all three pages when you want something changed in the header portion of your website, all you need to do is update `header.tpl`.

Inserting Dynamic Content

Let's add some more details to our website by displaying the current date and time at the headquarters of Smarty LLC. While we could use the same implementation we used above with the `include()` function, we will instead use the `insert()` function.

This function works in almost the same way as `include`, with a few important differences:

*   The results are not going to be cached by Smarty. This is an important detail in some circumstances, such as when you need to be absolutely sure that some portions of your templates are always dynamically generated.

- You are not actually including a file, but running a PHP function that you will need to provide. The name attribute is what tells Smarty what function it should call. For example, if you pass getCurrentTime to it, Smarty will call a function called smarty_insert_getCurrentTime.

You may also assign the output of this function to a template variable, and even call a special PHP script prior to executing it. Here's what our header.tpl file looks like now with the changes:

```
<html>
<head>
 <title>Smarty LLC</title>
</head>
<body>

<img src="images/new.gif">

{insert name="getCurrentTime" assign="current_time"
script="time_functions.inc.php"}

The current time is: {$current_time}
```

And the code for time_functions.inc.php is:

```
<?php
function smarty_insert_getCurrentTime()
{
    return gmdate('l, j F Y g:i a T');
}
?>
```

Here's what the front page of our website looks like now:

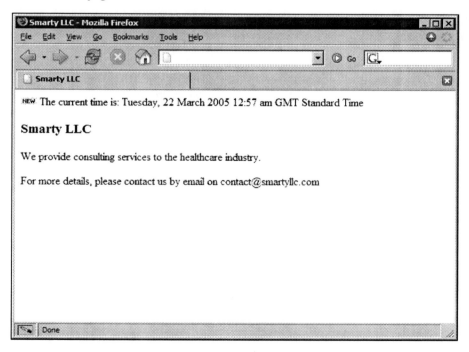

Passing Variables to Included Templates

Another very useful feature of the `include()` function is the ability to pass any number of arguments to the included templates. That allows you to include a template and override some default behavior when passing a flag to the inner template. So instead of having to display the current page title on each of our templates, let's create a new template file called `navigation.tpl` and use this special feature. Here are the contents of the new `navigation.tpl` file:

```
<h3>Smarty LLC{if $page_title != ''}: {$page_title}{/if}</h3>
```

Instead of simply using the include function to add the contents of this file to your other templates, we will also pass a variable to it. Here are the new contents of `index.tpl`:

```
{include file="header.tpl"}
{include file="navigation.tpl"}

<p>We provide consulting services to the healthcare industry.</p>

<p>For more details, please contact us by email on contact@smartyllc.com</p>

{include file="footer.tpl"}
```

Change the `about.tpl` template to the following:

```
{include file="header.tpl"}
{include file="navigation.tpl" page_title="Management Team"}

<p><b>Julian Fox, CEO</b> - Julian handles all management issues related to
the company, such as dealing with potential customers and providing a clear
strategy for services.</p>

<p><b>Ryan Foster, CTO</b> - Ryan handles all technical aspects of consulting
services available through Smarty LLC.</p>

{include file="footer.tpl"}
```

And change `contact.tpl` to have the following content:

```
{include file="header.tpl"}
{include file="navigation.tpl" page_title="Contact Us"}

<form method="post" action="contact_us.php">
<p>
 <b>Your Name:</b><br />
 <input type="text" name="name" size="40">
</p>

<p>
 <b>Your Email:</b><br />
 <input type="text" name="email" size="40">
</p>

<p>
 <b>Your Message:</b><br />
 <textarea name="message" cols="40" rows="10"></textarea>
</p>

<input type="submit" value="Send Message">
</form>

{include file="footer.tpl"}
```

Perform the same change across all other template files, and open the 'about' page in your browser. You should see something like the following:

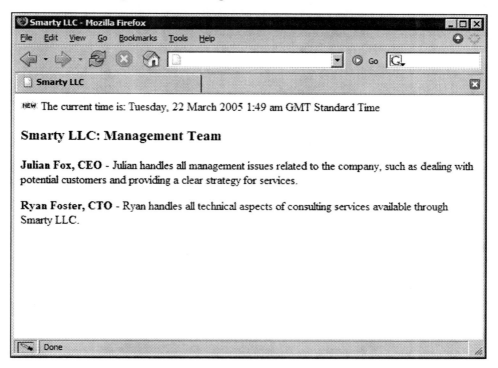

This looks exactly like what you had before, except that we are now modularizing our templates even more. The good thing now is that we can expand our new template with bread-crumb style navigation (that is, Home | Section | Sub-Section) in an easy way, by changing only one file.

Saving Variables in Configuration Files

It is extremely easy to pass variables to templates by using the normal PHP-based `assign()` function, like the following:

```php
<?php
include_once('libs/Smarty.class.php');
$smarty = new Smarty;

$smarty->assign('company_name', 'Smarty LLC');

$smarty->display('index.tpl');
?>
```

That would allow you to use the variable $company_name in your templates. While this is very handy, it doesn't make much sense to have that same line in each of your PHP scripts. Instead of duplicating PHP code, you can use Smarty configuration files to save variables and make them available to your templates.

A good example of the use of the {config_load} function is to translate your templates to several languages, but still keep one copy of your template structure for all of these separate sites.

Instead of having several copies of the same site structure, each having its own templates, but with hard-coded strings in each language, you can have just one site structure, and several configuration files, one for each language.

Create a file named english.conf and save the following content in it:

```
# global variables
company_name = "Smarty LLC"
```

Now change your existing navigation.tpl template file to this:

```
{config_load file="english.conf"}

<h3>{#company_name#}{if $page_title != ''}: {$page_title}{/if}</h3>
```

As you can see, you can use the variables saved in the configuration file directly in your templates.

Creating Configuration Sections for Each Page

While our existing english.conf file is pretty simple right now, it could grow quickly as we add more pages to our website, and as we translate each section of our site to separate languages. Instead of loading the entire configuration file as we did before, let's separate the variables of each page into sections, and load only the appropriate sections in our templates.

1. Modify the existing english.conf file to the following (the triple quotes are required for strings that span multiple lines):

    ```
    # global variables
    company_name = "Smarty LLC"

    [Index]
    intro_paragraph_1 = """We provide consulting services to the healthcare
    industry."""
    intro_paragraph_2 = """For more details, please contact us by email on
     contact@smartyllc.com"""
    ```

2. Change navigation.tpl back to the following:

    ```
    <h3>{#company_name#}{if $page_title != ''}: {$page_title}{/if}</h3>
    ```

3. Change index.tpl to the following:

    ```
    {config_load file="english.conf" section="Index"}
    {include file="header.tpl"}
    {include file="navigation.tpl"}

    <p>{#intro_paragraph_1#}</p>

    <p>{#intro_paragraph_2#}</p>

    {include file="footer.tpl"}
    ```

Firstly, notice how we pass the section name, in this case Index to the {config_load} function. This tells Smarty that we are only interested in the variables associated with that particular section. Also note that while we do specify the section, the global variable called company_name is still available in navigation.tpl. The reason is that this variable is global, and will always be available when that configuration file is loaded into the template.

The examples above set the configuration file manually to english.conf, but we could just as well expand on this and pass a variable to the template, and dynamically set the language of our website. It would be trivial to expand it even more and allow our visitors to choose the language of the site that they are interested in. Consider the following changes to navigation.tpl:

```
<p>
  Language:
  <a href="?language=en">English</a>  |
  <a href="?language=it">Italian</a>
</p>

<h3>{#company_name#}{if $page_title != ''}: {$page_title}{/if}</h3>
```

We are showing two links to our visitors, and allowing them to reload the current page with a query string, ?language=en or ?language=it. With some tweaks to our existing PHP code, we will switch languages on the fly:

```
<?php
include_once('libs/Smarty.class.php');
$smarty = new Smarty;

if (empty($_GET['language'])) {
    $smarty->assign('language', 'english');
} else {
    if ($_GET['language'] == 'en') {
        $smarty->assign('language', 'english');
    } elseif ($_GET['language'] == 'it') {
        $smarty->assign('language', 'italian');
    }
}

$smarty->display('index.tpl');
?>
```

Now change your existing index.tpl file to the following:

```
{config_load file="$language.conf" section="Index"}
{include file="header.tpl"}
{include file="navigation.tpl"}

<p>{#intro_paragraph_1#}</p>

<p>{#intro_paragraph_2#}</p>

{include file="footer.tpl"}
```

Let's see how this looks:

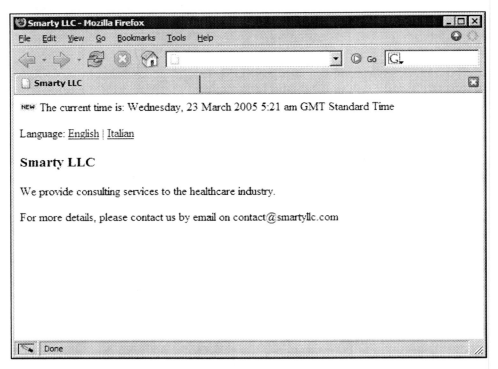

We are now dynamically selecting the appropriate language for the configuration file. You just got yourself an easy-to-maintain international website with a few simple steps!

Handling Lists in Templates

While our templates now handle a lot of custom functionality, such as content translated into several languages, and dynamically displaying the page title based on what value we pass when including another file, the site is still pretty static. That is, there isn't a lot of content on the site that is not known at the time that each particular page is requested.

Instead of hard-coding the list of available languages in navigation.tpl, let's dynamically generate the list of languages from a PHP array passed to the template.

1. Change index.php to the following:

    ```php
    <?php
    include_once('libs/Smarty.class.php');
    $smarty = new Smarty;

    if (empty($_GET['language'])) {
        $smarty->assign('language', 'english');
    } else {
        if ($_GET['language'] == 'en') {
    ```

```
        $smarty->assign('language', 'english');
    } elseif ($_GET['language'] == 'it') {
        $smarty->assign('language', 'italian');
    }
}

// list of available languages
$languages = array(
    'en' => 'English',
    'it' => 'Italian',
    'de' => 'German',
    'pt' => 'Portuguese'
);
$smarty->assign('languages', $languages);

$smarty->display('index.tpl');
?>
```

2. Now change navigation.tpl so that this array is processed and the HTML is dynamically generated according to the values we provide from the PHP script:

```
<p>
   Language:
{foreach from=$languages key="abbreviation" item="title"}
   <a href="?language={$abbreviation}">{$title}</a>  |
{/foreach}
</p>

<h3>{#company_name#}{if $page_title != ''}: {$page_title}{/if}</h3>
```

3. Open up our website in your browser, and you should now see something similar to this:

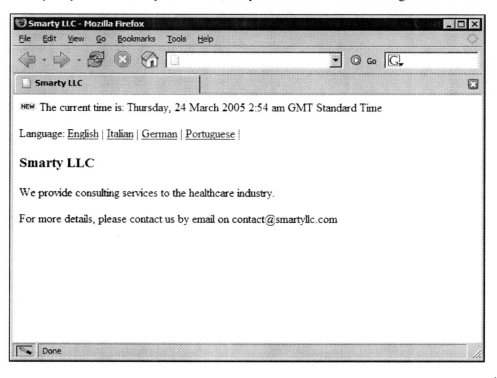

As you can see, the {foreach} function loops through the PHP array, and displays each of its options as a link on the page. The key attribute determines the name of the variable that will hold the key of the array element, and item will set the name of the variable that will hold the value.

There are several other attributes and features available through the {foreach} function. Notice how the list of languages on the previous screenshot ends with a space and the pipe character. Let's avoid adding those extra characters by using another feature of {foreach}.

1. Change navigation.tpl to include the following content:

    ```
    <p>
      Language:
    {foreach from=$languages key="abbreviation" item="title" name="lang"}
      <a href="?language={$abbreviation}">{$title}</a>
      {if not $smarty.foreach.lang.last}
       |
      {/if}
    {/foreach}
    </p>

    <h3>{#company_name#}{if $page_title != ''}: {$page_title}{/if}</h3>
    ```

2. Open your browser again on the website, and notice that the layout has changed:

108

There you go! The last white space and pipe characters are not being displayed anymore. By setting the `name` attribute on the `{foreach}` call, we are able to reference back to this loop from within your templates. The special variable `$smarty.foreach.lang` is how you refer to this loop, and the `last` attribute will tell you whether you are at the last iteration of the loop or not.

The code basically checks whether Smarty is processing the last iteration of the loop, and will output the space and pipe characters if that is not the case.

However, if you pay enough attention to details, you must have noticed that now the navigation links have an extra white space before all the pipe characters. This is basically a side effect of how we generated the HTML for the navigation links, which should look similar to the following:

```
<p>
  Language:
  <a href="?language=en">English</a>
      |
    <a href="?language=it">Italian</a>
      |
    <a href="?language=de">German</a>
      |
    <a href="?language=pt">Portuguese</a>
</p>
```

You see, browsers will render a white space before the non breaking space. We can fix that with yet another built-in Smarty function.

Removing Extra White Space from Templates

Let's change the `navigation.tpl` template again to remove the extra white space that ended up being displayed when we last modified our file.

1. Open the file `navigation.tpl` and change it to include the following content:

```
<p>
  Language:
{foreach from=$languages key="abbreviation" item="title" name="lang"}
  {strip}
  <a href="?language={$abbreviation}">{$title}</a>
  {if not $smarty.foreach.lang.last}
    |
  {/if}
  {/strip}
{/foreach}
</p>

<h3>{#company_name#}{if $page_title != ''}: {$page_title}{/if}</h3>
```

2. Reload the website again, and notice that the extra white spaces before the pipe characters are now gone:

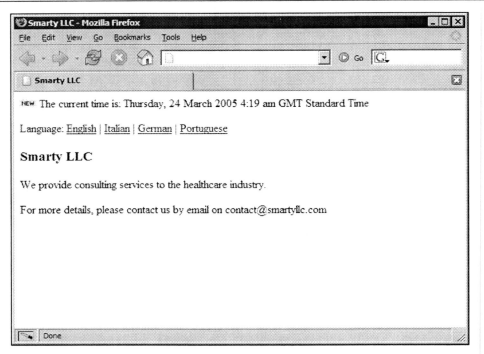

3. View the source of this page, and the navigation-related section should look something like this:

```
<p>
   Language:
   <a href="?language=en">English</a> |
<a href="?language=it">Italian</a> |
<a href="?language=de">German</a> |
<a href="?language=pt">Portuguese</a></p>
```

Notice how it's all in the same line now. The {strip} function is very useful for these types of cases in which white space matters in your pages, but it would be easier to maintain your website if you could still have it all on separate lines.

Handling JavaScript Code in Templates

It may seem like embedding JavaScript code in your templates might be straightforward, but a very important catch that you should be looking out for is that, since braces are used by Smarty as delimiters for function names and variables, something simple like creating a JavaScript function might result in a template parsing error. You can avoid this by following these steps.

Change header.tpl to the following:

```
<html>
<head>
 <title>Smarty LLC</title>
</head>
```

```
<body>
<script language="JavaScript">
<!--
function printMessage(str)
{
    alert(str);
}
//-->
</script>
<img src="images/new.gif">
{insert name="getCurrentTime" assign="current_time"
script="time_functions.inc.php"}
The current time is: {$current_time}
```

Reload any page of our website (since all of our templates include header.tpl in them), and you should see an error message similar to the following:

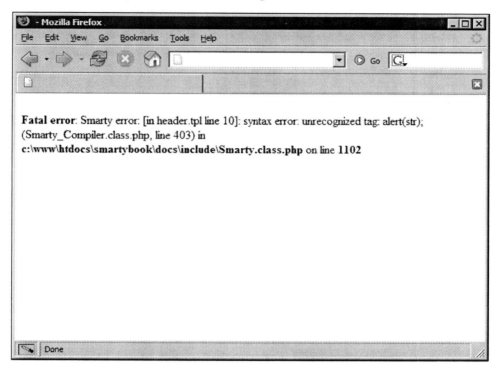

As you can see from the screenshot above, Smarty has a problem understanding that the function printMessage is something related only to the JavaScript code, and should be ignored. In order to fix this, there are two solutions using Smarty functions available to you:

- The combination of the functions {ldelim} and {rdelim}. The first one outputs the left template delimiter, and the last one outputs the right delimiter, which happen to be left and right braces. This is used by modifying header.tpl to use the {ldelim} and {rdelim} functions, as follows:

```
<html>
<head>
  <title>Smarty LLC</title>
</head>
<body>
  <script language="JavaScript">
  <!--
  function printMessage(str)
  {ldelim}
  alert(str);
  {rdelim}
  //-->
</script>
<img src="images/new.gif">
{insert name="getCurrentTime" assign="current_time"
script="time_functions.inc.php"}
The current time is: {$current_time}
```

- The {literal} block function, which tells Smarty to ignore anything found inside the tags, {literal} and {/literal}.

  We need to modify header.tpl like this to use the {literal} block function:

```
<html>
<head>
  <title>Smarty LLC</title>
</head>
<body>
{literal}
<script language="JavaScript">
<!--
function printMessage(str)
{
    alert(str);
}
//-->
</script>
{/literal}
<img src="images/new.gif">
{insert name="getCurrentTime" assign="current_time"
script="time_functions.inc.php"}
The current time is: {$current_time}
```

Changing the template using either of the options above will fix the Smarty parsing error, and our website should start working again.

Processing Deeply Nested Arrays

While the {foreach} function is perfect for handling PHP associative arrays, the {section} function is aimed at processing deeply nested arrays, or normal indexed arrays. Let's expand our page that describes the management team of our company by passing a deeply nested array describing each of the team members. This can be done by following these steps:

1. Change the existing index.php to the following:

```
<?php
include_once('libs/Smarty.class.php');
$smarty = new Smarty;

if (empty($_GET['language'])) {
    $smarty->assign('language', 'english');
} else {
```

```
        if ($_GET['language'] == 'en') {
            $smarty->assign('language', 'english');
        } elseif ($_GET['language'] == 'it') {
            $smarty->assign('language', 'italian');
        }
    }

    $team = array(
        0 => array(
                'name'  => 'Julian Fox', // crazy like a fox!
                'title' => 'CEO',
                'description' => 'Julian handles all management issues related to
                                the company, such as dealing with potential
                                customers and providing a clear strategy
                                for services.',
            ),
        1 => array(
                'name'  => 'Ryan Foster',
                'title' => 'CTO',
                'description' => 'Ryan handles all technical aspects of
                                consulting services available through
                                Smarty LLC',
            ),
        2 => array(
                'name'  => 'Adam Salsbury', // he will sell you anything!
                'title' => 'VP Sales',
                'description' => 'Adam is the person who closes our consulting
                                deals and handles all interactions with
                                existing customers.',
            ),
    );
    $smarty->assign('team', $team);

    // list of available languages
    $languages = array(
        'en' => 'English',
        'it' => 'Italian',
        'de' => 'German',
        'pt' => 'Portuguese'
    );
    $smarty->assign('languages', $languages);

    $smarty->display('about.tpl');
    ?>
```

2. And change the about.tpl template file to the following:

```
{config_load file="$language.conf" section="About"}
{include file="header.tpl"}
{include file="navigation.tpl" page_title="Management Team"}

{section name="i" loop=$team}
<p><b>{$team[i].name}, {$team[i].title}</b> - {$team[i].description}</p>
{/section}

{include file="footer.tpl"}
```

3.   Reload the management team page and see the results:

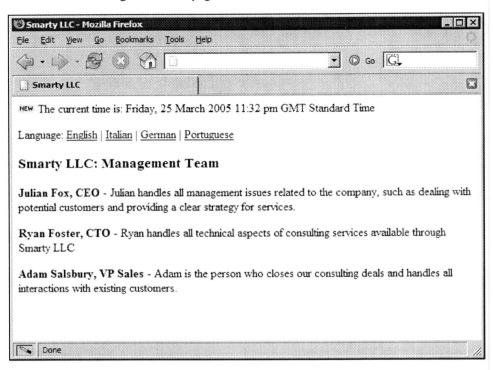

Voilà! You are now dynamically displaying the list of employees based on whatever you pass from the PHP script. The {section} function is similar to PHP's for construct, in that it loops through an array, and you can treat each of the elements in the array as an associative array. In our example above, we are looping through the list of employees, and using each key in the associative array to display the details of the employee, such as name, title, and description of what they do in the company.

You may also utilize most of the attributes available for the {foreach} function, such as last (as exemplified before) and more:

- start: This allows you to start iterating the given array from the specified position (the first element is zero).
- step: This allows you to set a custom step value, and skip certain values. For instance, if you set step to 3, the loop will process records 0, 3, 6 and so on.
- max: The maximum number of times that this loop will iterate.
- show: Whether to display the output of this function or not.
- index: Displays the current iteration, starting from zero.
- index_prev: Displays the previous iteration index, if any. It is set to -1 on the first iteration of the loop.

- `index_next`: Displays the next iteration index.
- `iteration`: Displays the current iteration index, starting from one.
- `first`: Set to true if the current iteration is the first one of the loop.
- `last`: Set to true if the current iteration is the last one of the loop.

However, instead of using `$smarty.foreach.foreach_name.last`, you will need to use `$smarty.section.section_name.last`, and so on. In order to better exemplify their usage, let's modify our management team template to display a number before the name of each employee.

Update the `about.tpl` file to contain the following:

```
{config_load file="$language.conf" section="About"}
{include file="header.tpl"}
{include file="navigation.tpl" page_title="Management Team"}
{section name="i" loop=$team}
<p><b>#{$smarty.section.i.iteration}: {$team[i].name}, {$team[i].title}</b> -
{$team[i].description}</p>
{/section}
{include file="footer.tpl"}
```

Reload the page in your browser, and you should see something like this:

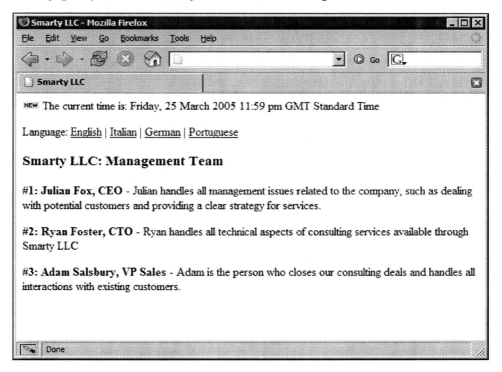

Cycling Through a List of Values

Another very convenient feature in Smarty is the ability to cycle through a pre-defined list of values with the {cycle} function. We are going to modify the management team template again, and display employees with alternating background colors.

Change your about.tpl file to include the following content:

```
{config_load file="$language.conf" section="About"}
{include file="header.tpl"}
{include file="navigation.tpl" page_title="Management Team"}
{section name="i" loop=$team}
{cycle assign="background_color" values="#F0F0F0,#DDDDDD"}
<p style="background: {$background_color};"><b>#{$smarty.section.i.iteration}:
{$team[i].name}, {$team[i].title}</b> - {$team[i].description}</p>
{/section}
{include file="footer.tpl"}
```

Reload the management team page and you should see the following:

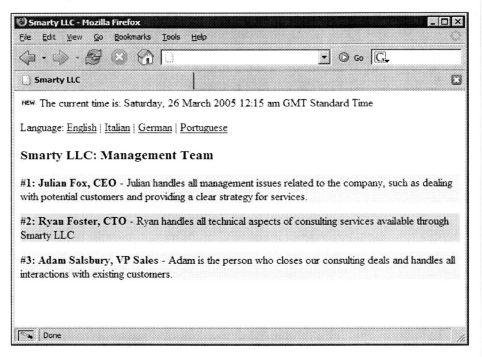

As you can see above, each call to {cycle} assigned a color to the $background_color variable by cycling through the available options, which should be separated by commas. In our example above, we used only two different colors (or values), but you could use as many as you want, and {cycle} will go through them all.

This is especially useful when you have a list of values such as search results to display, and want to make it easy for users to differentiate between one row of results and the next.

Avoiding Spam Indexers

A big problem nowadays on the Web is the epidemic of spam, ranging from pop-under advertisements to email-based messages that try to sell you anything from weight-loss solutions to stock tips. However, something that a lot of people don't realize is that just as Google crawls your website to add your content to its index, spam crawlers also look on your site for possible email addresses to send their junk to.

There are pretty reasonable business needs that dictate whether you need to display a contact email address on your website, and if you do, Smarty is there to help you with the {mailto} function.

This function allows you to encode an email address in such a way that spam crawlers cannot understand it as a real email address, but normal web browsers can.

Change the footer.tpl template file to the following:

```
<hr>
Copyright &copy; 2005 Smarty LLC<br />
Contact us at {mailto address="contact@smartyllc.com" subject="Smarty LLC
Contact" encode="javascript"}

</body>
</html>
```

Reload any of the pages on our website, and you should now see a new section of text on the bottom of the screen, as shown:

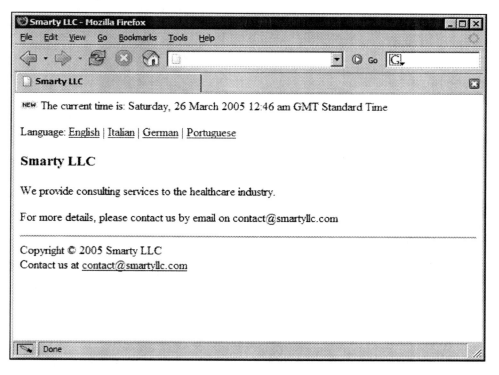

As you can see, it is simply displaying the email address to the browser. However, the real feature here is what is on the HTML code. The `footer.tpl` portion of HTML got changed to the following after Smarty processed it:

```
<hr>
Copyright &copy; 2005 Smarty LLC<br />
Contact us at <script type="text/javascript"
language="javascript">eval(unescape('%64%6f%63%75%6d%65%6e%74%2e%77%72%69%74%6
5%28%27%3c%61%20%68%72%65%66%3d%22%6d%61%69%6c%74%6f%3a%63%6f%6e%74%61%63%74%4
0%73%6d%61%72%74%79%6c%6c%63%2e%63%6f%6d%3f%73%75%62%6a%65%63%74%3d%53%6d%61%7
2%74%79%25%32%30%4c%4c%43%25%32%30%43%6f%6e%74%61%63%74%22%20%3e%63%6f%6e%74%6
1%63%74%40%73%6d%61%72%74%79%6c%6c%63%2e%63%6f%6d%3c%2f%61%3e%27%29%3b'))</scr
ipt>

</body>
</html>
```

The above will work just fine with browsers that support JavaScript, and spam crawlers will not be able to differentiate this block of JavaScript code from the rest of the HTML.

Form-Related Functions

We will now go over some of the other convenient functions that are very useful when handling form-related data, such as radio boxes, checkboxes, drop-down lists, and so on.

Let's start by creating a PHP script and a template file to handle a page that will allow our prospective customers to request a consulting quote. We will need to gather information such as their name, telephone number and the day, and a time for an initial appointment.

Here's the new `request.php` file:

```php
<?php
include_once('libs/Smarty.class.php');
$smarty = new Smarty;

if (empty($_GET['language'])) {
    $smarty->assign('language', 'english');
} else {
    if ($_GET['language'] == 'en') {
        $smarty->assign('language', 'english');
    } elseif ($_GET['language'] == 'it') {
        $smarty->assign('language', 'italian');
    }
}

// list of available languages
$languages = array(
    'en' => 'English',
    'it' => 'Italian',
    'de' => 'German',
    'pt' => 'Portuguese'
);
$smarty->assign('languages', $languages);

$smarty->display('request.tpl');
?>
```

And this is the template for this new page, to be named `request.tpl`:

```
{config_load file="$language.conf" section="Request"}
{include file="header.tpl"}
{include file="navigation.tpl" page_title="Request a Consulting Quote"}
```

```
<form method="post" action="request_quote.php">
<table border="1">
  <tr>
    <td bgcolor="{cycle values="#F0F0F0,#DDDDDD"}">Name:</td>
    <td><input type="text" name="full_name" size="40"></td>
  </tr>
  <tr>
    <td bgcolor="{cycle values="#F0F0F0,#DDDDDD"}">Phone Number:</td>
    <td><input type="text" name="phone" size="20"></td>
  </tr>
  <tr>
    <td bgcolor="{cycle values="#F0F0F0,#DDDDDD"}">
      Appointment Date and Time:
    </td>
    <td>
      {html_select_date display_years=false} 
      {html_select_time display_seconds=false minute_interval=15}
    </td>
  </tr>
  <tr>
    <td colspan="2" align="center">
      <input type="submit" value="Request">
    </td>
  </tr>
</table>
</form>

{include file="footer.tpl"}
```

It should look something like the following on your browser:

This is pretty straightforward. You can see that the call to {html_select_date} will end up displaying two different drop-down boxes, one so the user can select the month for the appointment, and another drop-down box for the day. The call to {html_select_time} also generated two drop-down boxes, one for the hour and the other for the minute.

However, notice that the call to {html_select_date} included a parameter display_years. If that parameter wasn't specified, yet another drop-down box would be displayed, this time listing years. Since our appointment form doesn't need to be that complicated, we set it to false.

Something similar also happened for the call to {html_select_time}. We passed a parameter display_seconds with the value of false to stop Smarty from displaying a drop-down box to select the seconds. Also, we set minute_interval to 15, so the options on the drop-down box end up being 00, 15, 30, and 45.

More Form-Related Functions

Let's expand our Request a Consulting Quote screen to ask prospective customers a few other questions, such as the type of consulting engagement, and payment option.

Change the request.php script to the following:

```php
<?php
include_once('Smarty.class.php');
$smarty = new Smarty;

if (empty($_GET['language'])) {
    $smarty->assign('language', 'english');
} else {
    if ($_GET['language'] == 'en') {
        $smarty->assign('language', 'english');
    } elseif ($_GET['language'] == 'it') {
        $smarty->assign('language', 'italian');
    }
}

// list of available consulting types
$smarty->assign('types', array(
    'custom'   => 'Custom Functions',
    'review'   => 'Code Review',
    'database' => 'Database Design',
));

// list of possible payment options
$smarty->assign('payment', array(
    'pre'    => 'Pre-paid',
    'aswego' => 'Pay as we go',
));

// list of available languages
$languages = array(
    'en' => 'English',
    'it' => 'Italian',
    'de' => 'German',
    'pt' => 'Portuguese'
);
$smarty->assign('languages', $languages);

$smarty->display('request.tpl');
?>
```

Modify the request.tpl template file so it contains the following:

```
{config_load file="$language.conf" section="Request"}
{include file="header.tpl"}
{include file="navigation.tpl" page_title="Request a Consulting Quote"}

<form method="post" action="request_quote.php">
<table border="1">
  <tr>
    <td bgcolor="{cycle values="#F0F0F0,#DDDDDD"}">Name:</td>
    <td><input type="text" name="full_name" size="40"></td>
  </tr>
  <tr>
    <td bgcolor="{cycle values="#F0F0F0,#DDDDDD"}">Phone Number:</td>
    <td><input type="text" name="phone" size="20"></td>
  </tr>
  <tr>
    <td bgcolor="{cycle values="#F0F0F0,#DDDDDD"}">
      Appointment Date and Time:
    </td>
    <td>
      {html_select_date display_years=false} 
      {html_select_time display_seconds=false minute_interval=15}
    </td>
  </tr>
  <tr>
    <td bgcolor="{cycle values="#F0F0F0,#DDDDDD"}">
      Consulting Type:
    </td>
    <td>{html_checkboxes name="type" options=$types separator="<br />"}</td>
  </tr>
  <tr>
    <td bgcolor="{cycle values="#F0F0F0,#DDDDDD"}">
      Payment Option:
    </td>
    <td>{html_radios name="payment" options=$payment selected="pre"}</td>
  </tr>
  <tr>
    <td colspan="2" align="center">
      <input type="submit" value="Request">
    </td>
  </tr>
</table>
</form>

{include file="footer.tpl"}
```

Reload the page in your web browser, and you should see something like the following:

There are several interesting features in this template:

- You can build a custom list of checkboxes just by passing a PHP array to the {html_checkboxes} function with the options parameter, and you can customize how the checkboxes are separated. We are using line breaks here to make it easier for our users to visualize the options of consulting types.

- You can also build a custom list of radio boxes in much the same way, and you can also set the radio box that should be selected by default by using the selected parameter to the {html_radios} function.

Summary

We covered the most important Smarty functions in this chapter, such as {section}, {foreach}, {literal}, {strip}, and {cycle}, while building a somewhat complex website by starting from a simple set of pages with not much content, and then gradually adding more information and features to our fantasy Smarty LLC company website.

You should now be able to use most Smarty functions comfortably in your own templates, by following the examples available throughout this chapter. Please try to remember that no matter what you need to do in your templates, there is probably somebody else who also needed to do the same, so a built-in Smarty function or even a plug-in might be available to do what you want.

Be sure to always check the Smarty documentation or the appropriate mailing lists. Smarty was designed from the ground up to be easy for template designers like yourself to use, so there's a big probability that what you need to do is already covered in the documentation. Also, there are lots of good people that help out on Smarty-related mailing lists, so make sure to give it a try.

7
Debugging for Designers

A basic fact for computing projects is that sooner, or later, things will inevitably go wrong. The same is true for template designers, obviously, so understanding common problems and ways to overcome them is a very important topic. While errors such as logical problems on your template code are typically semantic, others are related to things like typographical errors on a template filename that you are trying to include, or even forgetting to close a Smarty tag.

In this chapter, you will learn how to troubleshoot common Smarty errors, and logical or semantic problems on your templates, and how to quickly get over these issues and get your productivity back. We will do that together by building a small set of pages, and fixing problems as they occur.

Debugging Smarty Templates

Error messages are not usually displayed to users when something goes wrong with their templates, because of the way Smarty is designed. Since Smarty parses templates and compiles them into PHP scripts, your PHP configuration dictates whether error or warning messages will be displayed to the user's browser. This is usually a very good thing as it will hide any problems that might be found on your templates, but it will also prevent you from debugging problems.

Hence, the first thing that is needed in order to debug Smarty templates is to enable the proper configuration settings in PHP to display error messages. Whenever these settings are enabled, Smarty will start displaying debugging messages automatically.

The objective now is to find the php.ini configuration file and change the lines that set the following directives:

- error_reporting
- display_errors

The location of the php.ini file depends on the operating system that you are using (if you are developing locally), or the operating system of the server running your web pages. Usually, the file can be found on c:\WINDOWS\php.ini on Windows systems, and /etc/php.ini on UNIX systems. If you don't have access to this file, ask your system administrator for help.

You will need to change the two directives to the following:

- `error_reporting = E_ALL`
- `display_errors = On`

Save the file and restart your web server. To make sure that the settings were properly updated, create a PHP script named `phpinfo.php` with the following content:

```php
<?php
phpinfo();
?>
```

Search the output for these two directives, and check if they are enabled.

By changing the configuration as described above, you are changing PHP's global configuration and because of that, these changes will apply to any other site that runs off the same web server. If this is not appropriate for you, you can also manually override these directives by including the following PHP snippet on your scripts:

```php
<?php
ini_set('display_errors', 1);
error_reporting(E_ALL);
?>
```

After performing the changes above, your PHP pages should display error messages correctly for you. However, be sure to remember to disable these settings when you are ready to go live with your pages.

Semantic Errors

Let's start our first foray into template debugging by creating a simple PHP script and an accompanying Smarty template. It will serve as a contact form for a fictitious company, but it will be a good start for our examples. Here are the files:

Create a file called `index.php` and put the following content in it:

```php
<?php
include_once('libs/Smarty.class.php');
$smarty = new Smarty;

$departments = array(
    'marketing' => 'Marketing Department',
    'sales'     => 'Sales Department',
    'support'   => 'Customer Service Department'
);
$smarty->assign('departments', $departments);

$smarty->display('index.tpl');
?>
```

Create a new file called `index.tpl` with the following:

```html
<html>
<head>
<title>Example Corp.</title>
</head>
<body>
<h3>Example Corp. - Contact Us</h3>
```

```
<p>
  Please choose the department that you are trying to contact, and your
  contact details, and we will get back to you within 48 hours.
</p>

<form method="post" action="contact_handler.php">
<table border="1">
  <tr>
    <td><b>Department:</b></td>
    <td>
      {foreach key="name" item="description" from=$department}
      <input type="radio" name="dept" value="{$name}"> {$description}<br />
      {/foreach}
    </td>
  </tr>
  <tr>
    <td><b>Your Details:</b></td>
    <td>
      <input type="text" name="details" size="40">
    </td>
  </tr>
  <tr>
    <td colspan="2">
      <b>Message:</b><br />
      <textarea name="message" style="width: 100%;"></textarea>
    </td>
  </tr>
  <tr>
    <td colspan="2"><input type="submit" value="Send Message"></td>
  </tr>
</table>
</form>

</body>
</html>
```

After opening the PHP script on your web browser, your output should look like:

As you can see from the screenshot on the facing page, something is clearly wrong. The template code we created should iterate over the list of available departments, and print each as a different radio box. However, nothing is being displayed. In this case, we first check if the PHP script is passing the correct values to the template. We find that it is indeed passing an associative array of department names and their descriptions.

Next, we check if the Smarty template is using the proper variable name. Aha, there is indeed a problem here. The PHP script calls the list of department names $departments, but the Smarty template is using the unknown variable name $department instead. By changing the template file to reference the correct variable name, the actual department names will be displayed as shown:

Common Smarty Errors

Let's expand on our web page to maybe embed some JavaScript code on the page, so it can validate the values on the form prior to the user actually submitting them. The best way to do this is to trap the submission by setting an onsubmit JavaScript event handler on that form, and then checking the values from a function. Let's do that now by modifying the file index.tpl so that it contains the following:

```
<html>
<head>
<title>Example Corp.</title>
</head>
```

```
<body>

<h3>Example Corp. - Contact Us</h3>

<p>
   Please choose the department that you are trying to contact, and your
   contact details, and we will get back to you within 48 hours.
</p>

<script language="JavaScript">
<!--
function validateForm(f)
{
    if (f.details.value == '') {
        alert('Please enter your contact details.');
        return false;
    }
    return true;
}
//-->
</script>

<form method="post" action="contact_handler.php" onSubmit="return
validateForm(this);">
<table border="1">
   <tr>
      <td><b>Department:</b></td>
      <td>
        {foreach key="name" item="description" from=$departments}
        <input type="radio" name="dept" value="{$name}"> {$description}<br />
        {/foreach}
      </td>
   </tr>
   <tr>
      <td><b>Your Details:</b></td>
      <td>
        <input type="text" name="details" size="40">
      </td>
   </tr>
   <tr>
      <td colspan="2">
        <b>Message:</b><br />
        <textarea name="message" style="width: 100%;"></textarea>
      </td>
   </tr>
   <tr>
      <td colspan="2"><input type="submit" value="Send Message"></td>
   </tr>
</table>
</form>

</body>
</html>
```

This should be enough to trap the submission of the form when visitors forget to fill out their own contact information. Let's see what it looks like on the browser:

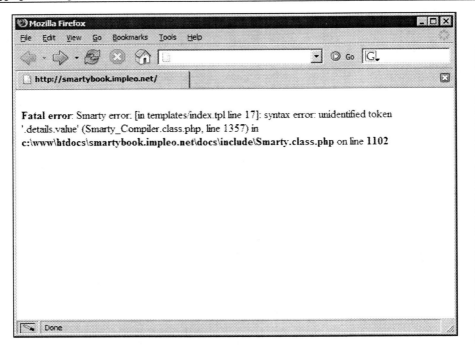

Oops, looks like something is wrong again. Notice, however, that this time there's actually some useful information displayed above. To begin with, we have a line number this time, so we can go directly to the template file and see what the problem is. Open index.tpl and go to the line number in which the error is indicated. It should look like this:

```
9   <p>
10    Please choose the department that you are trying to contact, and your
11    contact details, and we will get back to you within 48 hours.
12  </p>
13
14  <script language="JavaScript">
15  <!--
16  function validateForm(f)
17  {
18      if (f.details.value == '') {
19          alert('Please enter your contact details.');
20          return false;
21      }
22      return true;
23  }
24  //-->
25  </script>
26
27  <form method="post" action="contact_handler.php" onsubmit="return validateForm(this);">
28  <table border="1">
29    <tr>
```

As you can see from the screenshot from my text editor above, line 17 is part of the JavaScript code that we just added to this template. The problem here is that we forgot to tell Smarty not to parse this block of the template for variables or normal template syntax, so Smarty thinks that the left brace is telling it to parse the JavaScript code, which gives us this nonsensical error message.

In order to fix this, add {literal} before the <script> tag, and add {/literal} after the closing </script> tag.

After making these changes, try opening the page again. The page should now work and look like the following:

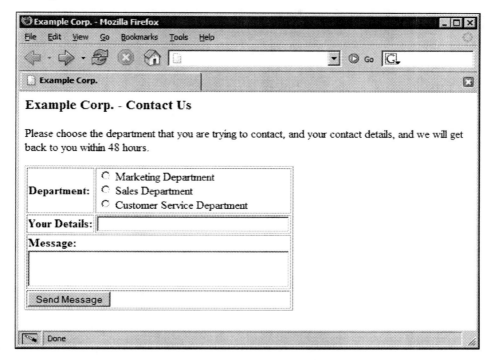

The lesson here is to be careful when using braces on your HTML, since it is a character that means something important to Smarty. If you need to have normal braces on your pages, use {literal} to tell Smarty to ignore those portions of the page.

Now let's add another feature to our contact form, so that we have a radio button that defaults to being checked when a visitor opens the page. We will simply change the template file, and manually check on the {foreach} loop if we should check the radio button or not.

Open index.tpl again and put the following content in it:

```
<html>
<head>
<title>Example Corp.</title>
</head>
<body>

<h3>Example Corp. - Contact Us</h3>

<p>
  Please choose the department that you are trying to contact, and your
```

```
    contact details, and we will get back to you within 48 hours.
</p>

{literal}
<script language="JavaScript">
<!--
function validateForm(f)
{
    if (f.details.value == '') {
        alert('Please enter your contact details.');
        return false;
    }
    return true;
}
//-->
</script>
{/literal}

<form method="post" action="contact_handler.php" onSubmit="return
validateForm(this);">
<table border="1">
  <tr>
    <td><b>Department:</b></td>
    <td>
      {strip}
      {foreach key="name" item="description" from=$departments}
      <input type="radio" name="dept" value="{$name}" {if $name ==
'marketing'}checked{/if}> {$description}<br />
      {/foreach}
    </td>
  </tr>
  <tr>
    <td><b>Your Details:</b></td>
    <td>
      <input type="text" name="details" size="40">
    </td>
  </tr>
  <tr>
    <td colspan="2">
      <b>Message:</b><br />
      <textarea name="message" style="width: 100%;"></textarea>
    </td>
  </tr>
  <tr>
    <td colspan="2"><input type="submit" value="Send Message"></td>
  </tr>
</table>
</form>

</body>
</html>
```

Now open your web browser again and see how it looks. The output will be something like this:

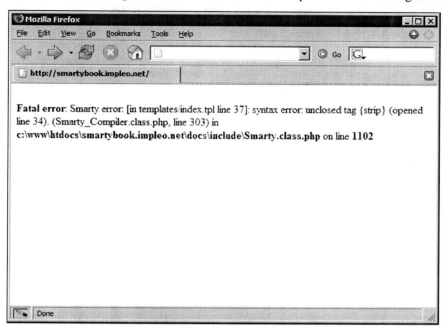

As you can see, one of our changes introduced a bug in the template that triggered this error message. Looks like we forgot to close the {strip} function with a {/strip} tag, hence the error above.

Let's fix the error message by changing index.tpl to the following:

```
<html>
<head>
<title>Example Corp.</title>
</head>
<body>

<h3>Example Corp. - Contact Us</h3>

<p>
  Please choose the department that you are trying to contact, and your
  contact details, and we will get back to you within 48 hours.
</p>

{literal}
<script language="JavaScript">
<!--
function validateForm(f)
{
    if (f.details.value == '') {
        alert('Please enter your contact details.');
        return false;
    }
    return true;
}
//-->
</script>
{/literal}
```

```
<form method="post" action="contact_handler.php" onSubmit="return
validateForm(this);">
<table border="1">
  <tr>
    <td><b>Department:</b></td>
    <td>
      {strip}
      {foreach key="name" item="description" from=$departments}
      <input type="radio" name="dept" value="{$name}" {if $name ==
'marketing'}checked{/if}> {$description}<br />
      {/foreach}
      {/strip}
    </td>
  </tr>
  <tr>
    <td><b>Your Details:</b></td>
    <td>
      <input type="text" name="details" size="40">
    </td>
  </tr>
  <tr>
    <td colspan="2">
      <b>Message:</b><br />
      <textarea name="message" style="width: 100%;"></textarea>
    </td>
  </tr>
  <tr>
    <td colspan="2"><input type="submit" value="Send Message"></td>
  </tr>
</table>
</form>

</body>
</html>
```

We simply added {/strip} after the {/foreach} tag. Now let's see if the error message goes away:

Beautiful, we should be good to go!

Other Common Smarty Errors

While the errors above are pretty common, the following are not the kind of errors related to your template coding practices, nor PHP configuration settings. Rather, they are related to system configuration issues, like permission bits being insufficient to open a file or a directory.

- **Warning: Smarty error: unable to read resource: "extra.tpl"**: In order to fix this type of error, make sure that the permission bits associated with the file are the appropriate ones for your website. That is, the web server that handles your pages needs to be able to access this file. Also, there might be a typo on the filename that causes this error.

- **Fatal error: Smarty error: unable to write to $compile_dir**: Smarty works with your templates by parsing them, and then it compiles the templates into PHP scripts to improve efficiency. That is, instead of having to parse the template each time your PHP script is requested, it will compile the template into a PHP version of it, and skip the parsing routine. It will usually only re-compile the template if it needs to, such as when the template file is modified. The error message above is related to this feature. The compiled templates directory (referenced as $compile_dir within Smarty) which is usually called templates_c needs to be configured in such a way that the web server is allowed to write new files to it. To fix this error, set the proper permission bits to the templates_c sub-directory.

Smarty Debug Console

Another very interesting Smarty feature that is relevant to template designers is the **Debug Console**. This is a feature that is totally informational, which can be used to debug problems on your templates. It's important to note that the Debug Console will only work when the display() function call is used for a template. If the PHP script is using fetch() instead to grab the HTML output, Smarty will not include the Debug Console on that.

In order to enable this feature, you will need to update the index.php script we have created throughout this chapter. Here's what the new content of index.php is supposed to be:

```php
<?php
include_once('libs/Smarty.class.php');
$smarty = new Smarty;
$smarty->debugging = TRUE;

$departments = array(
    'marketing' => 'Marketing Department',
    'sales'     => 'Sales Department',
    'support'   => 'Customer Service Department'
);
$smarty->assign('departments', $departments);

$smarty->display(index.tpl');
?>
```

When the $smarty->debugging flag is set to TRUE, and you open your PHP script on your browser, a pop-up window will be opened automatically with the Debug Console, and it should look like this:

Make sure that your browser is not blocking pop-up windows from your website; otherwise the Debug Console will never be displayed.

Summary

Smarty provides a huge list of features that are designed to help you while creating your templates, but that comes at a price—complexity. While Smarty is a bit more complex than your usual templating engine, its features are well worth it. We covered a few of the most common Smarty problems, and quick ways to get past them.

While you create your templates, keep in mind that the more complex they are the harder it will be to debug problems with them; so always strive to keep your templates as simple as possible. Whenever you need to debug something, remember to use the Debug Console if possible.

8

Built-in Smarty Variables and Methods

In order to understand Smarty variables and methods, let's first look at the Smarty library. Being a programmer probably makes you wonder how the Smarty library was built. If we look in the Smarty libs folder we can see four files: Config_File.class.php, debug.tpl, Smarty.class.php, and Smarty_Compiler.class.php.

The Config_File.class.php file contains a class for reading Smarty configuration files from the config folder. It has four configuration variables that you can edit to suit your application. These are:

Configuration Variable	Application
var $overwrite = true;	Controls whether variables with the same name overwrite each other.
var $booleanize = true;	Controls whether config values of on/true/yes and off/false/no get converted to Boolean values automatically.
var $read_hidden = true;	Controls whether hidden config sections/vars are read from the file.
var $fix_newlines = true;	Controls whether or not to fix Mac or DOS formatted newlines. If it is set to true, \r or \r\n will be changed to \n.

The debug.tpl file is a template for formatting the debugging console. You can control the format for the debugging console as you wish by editing the debug.tpl file. Here's a snapshot of the debugging console for the example in Chapter 2:

The `smarty_Compiler.class.php` file contains the `Smarty_Compiler` class that is responsible for template compilation. Basically, what it does is to check the templates for Smarty syntax and transform it into PHP code.

The `smarty.class.php` file contains the Smarty class, which is the interesting part of the library, meaning that if we will take a good look at it and understand it we will be able to find the best solutions for what we need to do with it.

It has a configuration section, which is basically a declaration of the class's public members. You can either edit those members in the `smarty.class.php` file or you can address them when creating a new Smarty class to overwrite their content.

Smarty's public class members are also called built-in variables. It is always a good idea to keep those variables handy, printed in a table, as is pretty difficult and not recommended to memorize them all.

After the public member declaration, the Smarty class contains a set of functions that are the class public methods, also described as built-in methods.

Built-in Smarty Variables

We talked earlier in this book about Smarty folders, the defaults, and how they can be changed. They are contained in a few members of the Smarty class and they can be set with a very simple syntax, for example:

```
...
$smarty = new Smarty ;
$smarty->template_dir = 'templates' ;
...
```

Let's have a look at all the built-in variables and what they do.

$template_dir

This contains the name of the folder where templates are located. The default value of this variable is `templates` meaning that it will look for the templates in the `templates` folder located in the same folder as the executing PHP script, unless you specify a resource for the template. For extra protection, you can lock this template folder from being accessed by the public, using Basic HTTP authentication or Apache `mod_rewrite`.

$compile_dir

This contains the name of the folder where the PHP scripts resulting from template compilation will be written. The default value of this variable is `templates_c` located in the same folder as the executing PHP script. Since the compiled templates contain PHP code it's not a very risky directory, but you must be sure you have write access to this folder.

$config_dir

This contains the name of the folder used to store the configuration files used in the templates. The default value of this variable is `configs` located in the same folder as the executing PHP script. For extra protection, you can lock this folder from being accessed by the public, using Basic HTTP authentication or Apache `mod_rewrite`.

$plugins_dir

This contains the name of the folder where Smarty looks for the plug-ins that will be loaded. The default value of this variable is `plug-ins` in the SMARTY_DIR folder. If an absolute path to the plug-ins folder is not supplied, Smarty will first look for the folder contained in this variable in the SMARTY_DIR folder. If it's not found there, will look for it in the current working directory, then in each entry in the PHP include path. That's why, for best performance it is recommended to use an absolute path or a path relative to SMARTY_DIR, else time is consumed in the search of the plug-ins folder when we need to load a plug-in.

$debugging

This is a Boolean variable that enables or disables the debugging console. The default value of this variable is `false` and it is not recommended to set it to `true` globally, especially in the production environment.

$error_reporting

When this variable contains a non-null value, the value will be used as PHP's `error_reporting-level` inside `display()` and `fetch()`. If debugging is enabled, this variable has no effect.

$debug_tpl

This contains the name of the template use for formatting the debugging console. The default is `debug.tpl` located in the `SMARTY_DIR` folder.

$debugging_ctrl

This determines whether debugging can be enabled from the browser. It has two possible values:

- **NONE**: This is the default value and means that no alternative way to enable debugging is allowed except through the `$debugging` variable.
- **URL**: This allows debugging to be enabled via the web browser. When the variable has this value, you can enable the debugging console by using `SMARTY_DEBUG` in the URL like `http://127.0.0.1/index.php?SMARTY_DEBUG`.

If the `$debugging` variable is set to true, the value of this variable is ignored.

$compile_check

This is a Boolean variable that tells Smarty whether or not to check if a template has modified its content. The default value of the variable is `true`, which means that Smarty will check to see if a template has changed its timestamp from the last compilation. If it has, Smarty will recompile that template. If you set the variable to `false`, Smarty will only compile a template upon it's first invocation and will not recompile it, irrespective of if you modified it or not. Setting the variable to `false` will improve performance on a project that doesn't change (for example, when going into production).

If caching is enabled and `$compile_check` is set to `true`, the cache files will be regenerated at every modification of the templates or configuration files involved.

$force_compile

This is a Boolean variable that tells Smarty if you want to compile the template every time it is invoked. This variable overrides the `$compile_check` variable. The default value is `false` and when it is set to `true`, the templates will be compiled upon every invocation, which can be useful for debugging and development. If caching is enabled, the cache files will be regenerated every time.

$caching

This is an integer variable that tells Smarty whether or not to cache the output of the templates. The variable has three possible values.

- **0**: This is the default value and it disables template caching.
- **1**: Enables caching and tells Smarty to use the variable `$cache_lifetime` in the Smarty class to determine if the cache has expired, meaning that it will check the validity of the cache by using the current value of `$cache_lifetime`.

- **2**: Enables caching and tells Smarty to use the variable `$cache_lifetime` in the cache file to determine if the cache has expired, meaning that it will check the validity of the cache by using the value of `$cache_lifetime` at the time when the cache files were created.

$cache_dir

This contains the name of the folder where template caches are stored. The default is `cache` in the same folder as the executing PHP script. For extra protection, you can lock this template folder from being accessed by the public, using Basic HTTP authentication or Apache `mod_rewrite`.

$cache_lifetime

This is an integer variable that contains the number of seconds that a template cache is valid. The default value of the variable is 3600, meaning that template caches expire in one hour. Using 0 as `$cache_lifetime` value tells Smarty to always regenerate the cache. This is good only for testing and development, not to disable caching as it will consume system resources to regenerate the cache (while `$caching = 'false'` won't). A value of -1 tells Smarty never to regenerate the cache.

$cache_modified_check

This is a Boolean variable only used when caching is enabled. The default value is `false`, but if it is set to `true`, Smarty will respect the `If-Modified-Since` headers sent from the client. In this case, if the cached file was not regenerated since the last visit, a 304 `Not Modified` header will be sent instead of the content. The cached content must not include `insert` tags.

$php_handling

This is a variable that tells Smarty how to handle PHP code between `<?php ... ?>` tags in the templates. The variable has four possible values that don't affect the PHP code between `{php}` and `{/php}` tags in the template. These are:

- `SMARTY_PHP_PASSTHRU`: This is the default value and means that Smarty will print tags as plain text.
- `SMARTY_PHP_QUOTE`: Smarty will quote tags as HTML entities.
- `SMARTY_PHP_REMOVE`: Smarty will remove tags from templates.
- `SMARTY_PHP_ALLOW`: Smarty will execute the PHP tags as PHP code.

$security

This is a Boolean variable that enables or disables template security features. The default value of this variable is `false` and when it is set to `true`, many things are restricted in templates that normally would go unchecked. Enabling template security is good when you have untrusted parties uploading or editing templates (for example, via FTP) because it reduces the risk of compromising the system through the template language. Unless the variable `$security_settings` specifies other things, enabling security gives you the following features:

- $php_handling is overwritten to SMARTY_PHP_PASSTHRU if it was set to SMARTY_PHP_ALLOW.
- PHP functions are not allowed in IF statements, except those that are specified in $security_settings.
- Templates can be included only from folders listed in the $secure_dir array.
- Local files can be accessed only from folders included in the $secure_dir array using {fetch}.
- The tags {php}, {/php} are not allowed in templates.
- Smarty will not accept PHP functions as modifiers, except any that are specified in $security_settings.

$secure_dir

This is an array of folders that contain templates considered secure. The value of $template_dir is implicitly in this array. When security is enabled, {include} and {fetch} will use this variable to access templates and files.

$security_settings

This is an array used to specify security settings when security is enabled. The array contains:

- **PHP_HANDLING**: The default is false. If it is set to true the $php_handling variable is not checked.
- **IF_FUNCS**: An array of PHP functions allowed in IF statements. The default PHP functions allowed are array, list, isset, empty, count, sizeof, in_array, is_array, true, and false.
- **INCLUDE_ANY**: The default is false. If it is set to true, $security_dir is ignored, meaning that templates can be included from anywhere.
- **PHP_TAGS**: The default is false. If it is set to true the {php}{/php} tags are allowed in templates.
- **MODIFIER_FUNCS**: An array containing the names of PHP functions allowed as modifiers. The default is an array containing count.

$trusted_dir

This is an array containing the names of the folders where trusted PHP scripts reside. The variable has effect only when security is enabled and contains the paths to the PHP scripts that can be executed directly from templates using {include php}.

$left_delimiter

This is a variable containing the left delimiter used by the template language. The default is {.

$right_delimiter

This is a variable containing the right delimiter used by the template language. The default is }.

$request_vars_order

This contains the order in which the request variables are registered. This variable is similar to the variables_order variable in php.ini. The default is EGPCS where E means environment, G means get, P means post, C means cookies, S means server.

$request_use_auto_globals

This is a Boolean variable that indicates whether $HTTP_*_VARS[] are used as request-vars or $_*[] vars. The default is false which means that $HTTP_*_VARS[] are used. If it is set to true, the variable $request_vars_order has no effect; instead gpc_order from php.ini is used. This variable affects templates that use {smarty.request.*}, {smarty.get.*}, and so on.

$compile_id

This is a string variable used for different sets of compiled files for the same template. This is useful for internationalization. Instead of creating different sets of templates for each language you can set different compile_ids like en, fr, and so on.

$use_sub_dirs

This is a Boolean variable that tells Smarty whether or not to use sub-directories in the $cache_dir and $compile_dir folders. The default value of this variable is false. Sub-directories are better organized but may not work if PHP safe mode is enabled.

$default_modifiers

This is an array containing a list of modifiers to apply to all template variables. The default is a null array, but if you want, for example to HTML-escape all variables by default, use array('escape:"htmlall"'). If you want a variable not to go through the default modifiers, use the syntax {$var|smarty:nodefaults}.

$default_resource_type

This tells Smarty what resource type to use when one is not specified at the beginning of resource path. For example:

```
$smarty->display('file:index.tpl'); // will use file resource type
$smarty->display('db:index.tpl'); // will use database resource type
$smarty->display('index.tpl'); // will use the default resource type
```

The same happens with {include file = 'file:index.tpl'}.

The default value of this variable is file.

$cache_handler_func

This specifies the function used for file caching. The default is null, which means the default (built-in) caching function is used.

143

$autoload_filters

This is an array containing a list of filters that Smarty should automatically load. The default is an empty array.

$config_overwrite

This is a Boolean variable that tells Smarty whether to overwrite configuration file variables with the same name or not. The default value of this variable is `true`. If it is set to `false` the variables with the same name will be pushed into an array.

$config_booleanize

This is a Boolean variable that tells Smarty whether to automatically booleanize configuration file variables. The default is `true`, meaning that every variable containing a value of `on`, `off`, `yes`, `no`, `true`, or `false` will automatically be converted to the Boolean variable type.

$config_read_hidden

This is a Boolean variable that tells Smarty if hidden sections (sections beginning with a period) in the configuration files can be read by templates. The default is `false` because the point of hidden sections is that the application can read them but the templates can't.

$config_fix_newlines

This is a Boolean variable that tells Smarty whether or not to convert Mac and DOS newline characters (\r or \r\n) to \n when they are parsed. The default value of this variable is `true`.

$default_template_handler_func

This contains the name of a PHP function that will be executed if a template cannot be found from its resource.

$compiler_file

This is a variable that contains the name of the file in which the Smarty compiler class resides. The value can be a full pathname or relative to the `php_include` path. The default value of this variable is `Smarty_Compiler.class.php`.

$compiler_class

This contains the name of the class used for compiling templates. The default value of this variable is `Smarty_Compiler`.

$config_class

This contains the class used to load configuration variables. The default value of this variable is `Config_File`.

Handy Built-in Smarty Variables Table

After having a look at all the variables and what they do, we will present all these variables in a table with their defaults and a small explanation.

Having the built-in Smarty variables in a table is always handy, especially for beginners and intermediate users. Only after using Smarty for long enough, will you be able to memorize most of these variables, but even then you can keep a printed table of the variables to look for what you need faster.

Variables	Description
var $template_dir = 'templates';	The name of the directory where templates are located.
var $compile_dir = 'templates_c';	The directory where compiled templates are located.
var $config_dir = 'configs';	The directory where config files are located.
var $plug-ins_dir = array('plug-ins');	An array of directories searched for plug-ins.
var $debugging = false;	If debugging is enabled, a debug console window will display when the page loads (make sure your browser allows pop-ups).
var $error_reporting = null;	When set, Smarty uses this value as error_reporting-level.
var $debug_tpl = '';	This is the path to the debug console template. If not set, the default one will be used.
var $debugging_ctrl = 'NONE';	This determines if debugging can be enabled from the browser. NONE => no debugging control allowed. URL => enable debugging when SMARTY_DEBUG is found in the URL (for example, http://127.0.0.1/index.php?SMARTY_DEBUG).
var $compile_check = true;	This tells Smarty whether to check for recompiling or not. Recompiling does not need to happen unless a template or config file is changed. Typically you enable this during development, and disable it for production.
var $force_compile = false;	This forces templates to compile every time. Useful for development or debugging.
var $caching = 0;	This enables template caching. 0 = no caching 1 = use class cache_lifetime value 2 = use cache_lifetime in cache file
var $cache_dir = 'cache';	The name of the directory for cache files.
var $cache_lifetime = 3600;	This is the number of seconds cached content will persist. 0 = always regenerate cache -1 = never expires

Variables	Description
var $cache_modified_check = false;	Only used when $caching is enabled. If true, then If-Modified-Since headers are respected with cached content, and appropriate HTTP headers are sent. This way repeated hits to a cached page do not send the entire page to the client every time.
var $php_handling = SMARTY_PHP_PASSTHRU;	This determines how Smarty handles "<?php ... ?>" tags in templates. Possible values: SMARTY_PHP_PASSTHRU—print tags as plain text SMARTY_PHP_QUOTE—escape tags as entities SMARTY_PHP_REMOVE—remove php tags SMARTY_PHP_ALLOW—execute php tags
var $security = false;	This enables template security. When enabled, many things are restricted in the templates that normally would go unchecked. This is useful when untrusted parties are editing templates and you want a reasonable level of security. (no direct execution of PHP in templates for example).
var $secure_dir = array();	This is the list of template directories that are considered secure. This is used only if {@link $security} is enabled. One directory per array element. {@link $template_dir} is in this list implicitly.
var $security_settings = array('PHP_HANDLING' => false, 'IF_FUNCS' => array('array', 'list', 'isset', 'empty', 'count', 'sizeof', 'in_array', 'is_array', 'true', 'false'), 'INCLUDE_ANY' => false, 'PHP_TAGS' => false, 'MODIFIER_FUNCS' => array('count'), 'ALLOW_CONSTANTS' => false);	These are the security settings for Smarty. They are used only when {@link $security} is enabled.
var $trusted_dir = array();	This is an array of directories where trusted PHP scripts reside. {@link $security} is disabled during their inclusion/execution.
var $left_delimiter = '{';	The left delimiter used for the template tags.
var $right_delimiter = '}';	The right delimiter used for the template tags.
var $request_vars_order = 'EGPCS';	The order in which request variables are registered, similar to variables_order in php.ini E = Environment, G = GET, P = POST, C = Cookies, S = Server.
var $request_use_auto_globals = true;	Indicates whether $HTTP_*_VARS[] (request_use_auto_globals=false) are used as request-vars or $_*[]-vars. note: if request_use_auto_globals is true, then $request_vars_order has no effect, but the php-ini-value "gpc_order" is used.

Variables	Description
var $compile_id = null;	Set this if you want different sets of compiled files for the same templates. This is useful for things like different languages. Instead of creating separate sets of templates per language, you set different compile_ids like 'en' and 'de'.
var $use_sub_dirs = false;	This tells Smarty whether or not to use sub-directories in the cache/ and templates_c/ directories. Sub-directories better organized, but may not work well with PHP safe mode enabled.
var $default_modifiers = array();	This is a list of the modifiers to apply to all template variables. Put each modifier in a separate array element in the order you want them applied. Example: <code>array('escape:"htmlall"');</code>
var $default_resource_type = 'file';	This is the resource type to be used when not specified at the beginning of the resource path. Examples: $smarty->display('file:index.tpl'); $smarty->display('db:index.tpl'); $smarty->display('index.tpl'); // will use default resource type {include file="file:index.tpl"} {include file="db:index.tpl"} {include file="index.tpl"} {* will use default resource type *}
var $cache_handler_func = null;	The function used for cache file handling. If not set, built-in caching is used.
var $autoload_filters = array();	This indicates which filters are automatically loaded into Smarty.
var $config_overwrite = true;	This determines if config file vars of the same name overwrite each other or not. If it is disabled, duplicated variables are accumulated in an array.
var $config_booleanize = true;	This determines whether or not to automatically booleanize config file variables. If enabled, then the strings "on", "true", and "yes" are treated as Boolean true, and "off", "false", and "no" are treated as Boolean false.
var $config_read_hidden = false;	This determines whether hidden sections [.foobar] are readable from the templates or not. Normally you would never allow this since that is the point behind hidden sections: the application can access them, but the templates cannot.
var $config_fix_newlines = true;	This determines whether or not to automatically fix newlines in config files. It basically converts \r (Mac) or \r\n (DOS) to \n
var $default_template_handler_func = '';	If a template cannot be found, this PHP function will be executed. Useful for creating templates on-the-fly or other special action.
var $compiler_file = 'Smarty_Compiler.class.php';	The file that contains the compiler class. This can be a full pathname, or relative to the php_include path.
var $compiler_class = 'Smarty_Compiler';	The class used for compiling templates.
var $config_class = 'Config_File';	The class used to load config vars.

Built-in Smarty Methods

Methods are the Smarty class public functions used for intercommunication between the application and the templates. We will explain now how they are built and the syntax of all methods, and in the next chapter we will discuss how to optimize the usage of those methods.

assign

```
void assign ( mixed var )
void assign ( string varname, mixed var )
```

The `assign` method is used to pass variables to templates. You can either pass pairs of name and value or an associative array containing name and value pairs.

```php
<?php
$smarty = new Smarty;
$website = 'http://www.packtpub.com';

// Pass pairs to template
$smarty->assign('publisher','Packt Publishing');
//or
$smarty->assign('website',$website);

// Pass an associative array
$smarty->assign(array("publisher" => "Packt Publishing", "website" =>
$website));
?>
```

The parameter `varname` is then used in the templates, for example:

```html
<html>
<body>
Publisher : <a href="{$website}"> {$publisher} </a>
</body>
</html>
```

assign_by_ref

```
void assign_by_ref ( string varname, mixed var)
```

The `assign_by_ref` method is used to pass values to templates by reference instead of creating a copy of the value and passing it as in the `assign` method. Referencing is a PHP method that is different from the C pointers method. In PHP, variables and content are different, so you can use different names for the same content. Modifying the content of a reference variable will modify the content of all variables that refer that content. For objectsit is better to use the `assign_by_ref` method because in this way you avoid making a copy of the object in memory, thus making things a bit faster.

The code shown next has the same effect for the template designer. However, the internal mechanism will not make a copy of the variable in memory like in the `assign` method, but if the template designer makes any modifications on the variable's content, the content will be modified in the `$website` variable in our PHP file.

```php
<?php
$smarty = new Smarty;
$website = 'http://www.packtbub.com';

$smarty->assign_by_ref('website',$website);
?>
```

Example: Working of assign and assign_by_ref

Let's see for ourselves how the `assign()` and `assign_by_ref()` methods work and what effect they have on the variables.

We will create a simple page, just to get the idea behind the `assign()` and `assign_by_ref()` methods. First, let's create a file named `index.php` in the document root of our server, like this:

```php
<?php

require("libs/Smarty.class.php");

$publisher='Packt Publishing';
$website = 'http://www.packtpub.com';

$smarty = new Smarty;

$smarty->assign_by_ref('publisher',$publisher);
$smarty->assign('website',$website);

$smarty->display('index.tpl');

print ' <hr>
    <h3> Hello, I am index.php. First, I displayed the index.tpl template.
</h3>
    Now we will see what happened to the content our variables: <br>
    The $publisher variable was sent using <b> assign_by_ref </b> method
    and now contains <font color=red> '. $publisher .'</font><br>
    and the $website variable was sent using <b> assign </b> method
    and now contains <font color=red> '. $website ;

?>
```

Then, go to the `templates` folder and create a file named `index.tpl`, like this:

```html
<html>
<head> <title> Example of assign and assign_by_ref </title>
</head>

<body>

<h3> Hello, I am the template index.tpl and I say: </h3>

I received the value of variable $publisher :
    <font color="blue"> {$publisher} </font> <br>

I received the value of variable $website :
    <font color="blue"> {$website} </font> <br>
<br>

I will apply the UPPER modifier on both variables by doing : <br>

    <b> assign var="publisher" value=$publisher|upper </b> <br>
    <b> assign var="website" value=$website|upper </b> <br>

    {assign var="publisher" value=$publisher|upper}
    {assign var="website" value=$website|upper}
...Done ! <br>
    Now, $publisher is:
    <font color="blue"> <b> {$publisher} </b></font> <br>
```

```
and $website is
    <font color="blue"> <b> {$website} </b></font> <br>

<h3> End of Template index.tpl </h3>
```

How it Works

We have created a file index.php in which we have two variables—$publisher and $website. They contain the values Packt Publishing and http://www.packtpub.com.

We will assign the first variable ($publisher) by reference to the templates and the second ($website) normally using the assign() method. Next, we will display index.tpl, which will print the content of the variables received from index.php. After that, the variables will be modified using the upper modifier:

```
{assign var="publisher" value=$publisher|upper}
{assign var="website" value=$website|upper}
```

The content of the variables is printed again. This ends index.tpl, so index.php will continue to execute.

The next command in index.php is to print the content of the $publisher and $website variables. We will see that the variable sent by reference modified its value while the other didn't, because a copy of its content was modified and not the actual content of the variable.

The Result

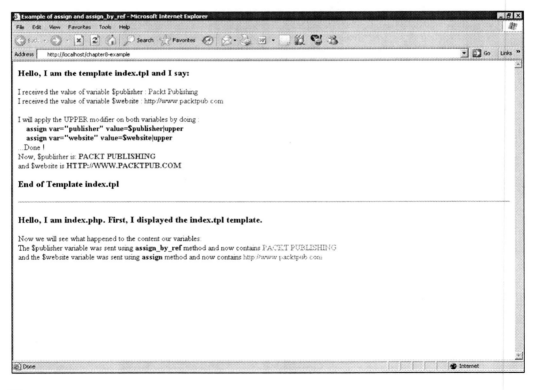

Just as we expected, the content of the $publisher variable, which was sent to the template using assign_by_ref() method, changed to PACKT PUBLISHING, and the content of the $website variable was not modified, even if it was modified in the template, because it was sent using the assign() method.

append

```
void append ( mixed var)
void append ( string varname, mixed var [, bool merge])
```

This method is used to append an element to an assigned array. If varname is not an array it will be converted to array and then the element appended to it. You can either pass pairs of name and value or an associative array containing name and value pairs as in the assign method. The optional parameter merge is false by default and if it is set to true the value will be merged with the array, not appended. Please note that this is different from the array_merge() function in PHP, which, in the case of numerically indexed arrays wipes out the numerical keys and renumbers them. Merging numerically indexed arrays with this method may result in non-sequential keys, and hence it's not recommended.

```php
<?php
$smarty = new Smarty;
$website = 'http://www.packtpub.com';

// Append pairs
$smarty->append("publisher","Packt Publishing");
//or
$smarty->append("website",$website);

// Append an associative array
$smarty->append(array("publisher" => "Packt Publishing", "website" =>
$website));
?>
```

append_by_ref

```
void append_by_ref ( string varname, mixed var [, bool merge])
```

This method is used to append values to assigned arrays by reference. This method has the same effect as the append() method except that instead of sending a copy of the content of the variable it will send a reference of the content.

clear_assign

```
void clear_assign ( mixed var)
```

This method is used to clear the value of an assigned variable. Parameters can be either the name of a variable or an array containing a list of variable names.

```php
<?php
...
//clear a single variable
$smarty->clear_assign("publisher");

//clear more variables
$smarty->clear_assign(array("publisher","website"));
...
?>
```

register_function

```
void register_function ( string name, mixed impl [, bool cacheable [, mixed
cache_attrs]])
```

This method dynamically registers template function plug-ins. The parameters are the name of the function used in templates, the name of the PHP function that implements the plug-in, a Boolean parameter, which specifies whether or not this plug-in is cacheable, and an array of attribute names that should be cached.

The `impl` parameter can be:

- A string containing the name of a PHP function
- An array of the form `array(&$object, $method)` with `&$object` being a reference of an object and `$method` a method of that object
- An array of the form `array(&$class, $method)` with `$class` being a class name and `$method` a method of that class

```php
<?php
...
$smarty->register_function("copyright","print_copyright");

function print_copyright($params)
{
    $year = params ['year'];
    return('© Copyright '. $year .' Packt Publishing. All rights reserved');
}
...
?>
```

Now, from the templates we can use the following to print © Copyright 2005 Packt Publishing. All rights reserved

```
{copyright year="2005"}
```

unregister_function

```
void unregister_function ( string name)
```

This method is used to dynamically unregister a template function plug-in. It has only one parameter, which is the template function name. For example:

```
<?php
...
$smarty->unregister_function("assign");
...
?>
```

will not allow template designers to use the `assign()` function.

register_object

```
void register_object ( string object_name, object object,
array allowed_methods_properties, boolean format, array block_methods)
```

This method is used to register an object that will be used in templates. The method's parameters are:

- **object_name**: The name of the template object.
- **object**: This is a reference to the PHP object.
- **allowed_methods_properties**: An array containing a list with the object's allowed methods. If the array is empty, all methods will be allowed.
- **format**: A Boolean variable that specifies whether the arguments will be in Smarty format or traditional.
- **block_methods**: An array containing methods that should be treated as blocks, meaning they will have a closing tag in the template, e.g. {object->method} ... {/object->method}. It only has effect if `format` is true.

unregister_object

```
void unregister_object ( string object_name)
```

This method unregisters template objects. The parameter is the template object's name.

register_block

```
void register_block ( string name, mixed impl, [bool cacheable, [mixed
cache_attrs]])
```

This method is used to dynamically register block function plug-ins. The parameters are the same as for the `register_function` method, and the effect of this method is almost the same, except that this is a block function.

```
<?php
...
$smarty->register_block("ban","check_words");

function check_words($params , $content, &$smarty, &$repeat)
{
```

153

```
$bad_words = explode(" ",$params['words']);
$words = explode(" ",$content);
for($i=0; $i<sizeof($words); $i++)
{
    for($j=0; $j<sizeof($bad_words); $j++)
    if ( $words[$i] == $bad_words[$j] )
        {
            $words[$i] = 'XXXXX';
        }
}
$output = implode(" ",$words);
return $output;
}
...
?>
```

Now, we can use the block function plug-in like this:

```
{ban words="abc xyz"}
I think this abc has a nice xyz
{/ban}
```

This will output I think this XXXXX has a nice XXXXX.

unregister_block

```
void unregister_block ( string name)
```

This method is used to dynamically unregister a block function plug-in. The parameter is the block function name we need to unregister.

register_compiler_function

```
void register_compiler_function ( string name, mixed impl, [bool
cacheable])
```

This method is used to dynamically register a compiler function plug-in. Its parameters are the compiler function's name, the PHP function that implements it, and a Boolean parameter for caching, which is set to true by default.

The impl parameter can be:

- A string containing the name of a PHP function
- An array of the form array(&$object, $method) with &$object being a reference of an object and $method a method of that object
- An array of the form array(&$class, $method) with $class being a class name and $method a method of that class

unregister_compiler_function

```
void unregister_compiler_function ( string name)
```

This method is used to dynamically unregister a compiler function plug-in. The parameter is the compiler function's name.

register_modifier

```
void register_modifier ( string name, mixed impl)
```

This method is used to dynamically register a modifier plug-in. The first parameter is the name of the modifier and the second is the PHP function that implements the modifier. The `impl` parameter is similar to the `impl` parameter in the `register_compiler_function()` method.

```php
<?php
...
$smarty->register_modifier("len","strlen");
...
?>
```

Now if we use it in the templates, {var|len} will output the length of the string variable.

unregister_modifier

```
void unregister_modifier ( string name)
```

This method is used to dynamically unregister a modifier plug-in. The parameter is the name of the modifier plug-in to unregister.

register_resource

```
void register_resource ( string name, array resource_funcs)
```

This method is used to dynamically register a resource plug-in. The first parameter is the resource name and the second is an array of PHP functions implementing the resource. The `resource_funcs` must be an array of four or five elements. If the array has four elements, the elements represent function callbacks for `source`, `timestamp`, `secure`, and `trusted` and in the case of a 5-element array, the first element must be an object reference or a class name of the object or class implementing the resource, and the next four elements must be method names implementing `source`, `timestamp`, `secure`, and `trusted`.

```php
<?php
...
$smarty->register_resource("db", array("db_get_template",
"db_get_timestamp",
"db_get_secure",
"db_get_trusted"));
...
?>
```

unregister_resource

```
void unregister_resource ( string name)
```

This method is used to dynamically unregister a resource plug-in. The parameter is the name of the resource plug-in.

register_prefilter

```
void register_prefilter (mixed function)
```

This method is used to dynamically register a prefilter function to apply to a template before compiling. The parameter is the PHP function callback, which can be:

- A string containing the name of a PHP function
- An array of the form array(&$object, $method) with &$object being a reference of an object and $method a method of that object
- An array of the form array(&$class, $method) with $class being a class name and $method a method of that class

unregister_prefilter

```
void unregister_prefilter (string function_name)
```

This method is used to dynamically unregister a prefilter function. The parameter is the prefilter name.

register_postfilter

```
void register_postfilter (mixed function)
```

This method is used to dynamically register a postfilter function to apply to a compiled template after compilation. The parameter is the PHP function callback, which can be:

- A string containing the name of a PHP function
- An array of the form array(&$object, $method) with &$object being a reference of an object and $method a method of that object
- An array of the form array(&$class, $method) with $class being a class name and $method a method of that class

unregister_postfilter

```
void unregister_postfilter ( string function_name)
```

This method is used to dynamically unregister a postfilter function. The parameter is the postfilter name.

register_outputfilter

```
void register_outputfilter ( mixed function)
```

This method is used to dynamically register an output filter function to apply to a template output. The parameter is the PHP function callback, which can be:

- A string containing the name of a PHP function
- An array of the form array(&$object, $method) with &$object being a reference of an object and $method a method of that object
- An array of the form array(&$class, $method) with $class being a class name and $method a method of that class

unregister_outputfilter

```
void unregister_outputfilter ( string function_name)
```

This method is used to dynamically unregister an output filter function. The parameter is the outputfilter name.

load_filter

```
void load_filter ( string type, string name)
```

This method is used to load a filter plug-in of specified name and type. The first parameter can be pre for prefilters, post for post filters, or output for output filters. The second parameter is the name of the filter plug-in.

```php
<?php
...
// load the built-in outputfilter trimwhitespaces
$smarty->load_filter('output','trimwhitespaces');
...
?>
```

clear_cache

```
void clear_cache ( string template [, string cache_id [, string compile_id
[, int expire_time]]])
```

This method is used to clear the cached content for a certain template. The first parameter is the template name. The second optional parameter is the cache_id of the template in case of multiple caches. The third optional parameter is compile_id and the fourth represents the minimum age in seconds the cache must be before it will be cleared.

```php
<?php
...
// clear the cache for index.tpl
$smarty->clear_cache("index.tpl");

//clear the cache with cache id 1 in an multiple-cache template
$smarty->clear_cache("index.tpl","1");
...
?>
```

clear_all_cache

```
void clear_all_cache ( [int expire_time])
```

This method is used to clear the entire template cache (for all templates). It has an optional parameter, which specifies the minimum age in seconds the cache must be before it will be cleared.

is_cached

```
bool is_cached ( string template [, string cache_id [, string
compile_id]])
```

This method returns true if a valid cache is found for the template specified by the first parameter. If the template has multiple caches you can specify a cache_id optionally and/or a compile_id. If the is_cached method returns true, the cached content is loaded and stored internally. That means that display and fetch methods will return the cached output without trying to reload the cache file. Also, after is_cached has returned true, the clear_cache() method has no effect.

clear_all_assign

```
void clear_all_assign ( void )
```

This method will clear all the assigned template variables.

clear_compiled_tpl

```
void clear_compiled_tpl ( [string tpl_file [, string compile_id [, int
exp_time]]])
```

This method clears the compiled template of the specified template, or all compiled templates if one is not specified. If you pass the compile_id parameter, only the compiled template for this compile_id is cleared. The third optional parameter is the age in seconds that the compiled templates must be before clearing.

template_exists

```
bool template_exists ( string template)
```

This method checks whether the specified template exists or not. The parameter can be a resource string specifying a template or a path to the template in the file system.

get_template_vars

```
array get_template_vars ( [string varname])
```

This method will return an array containing all template variables values or the given assigned variable value.

```php
<?php
...
// get all assigned variables in an array
$variables = $smarty->get_template_vars();

// get the variable publisher
$publisher = $smarty->get_template_vars('publisher');
...
?>
```

get_config_vars

```
array get_config_vars ( [string varname])
```

This method will return an array containing all configuration variables values or the given assigned variable value.

trigger_error

```
void trigger_error ( string error_msg [, int level])
```

This method is used to output an error message using Smarty. The first parameter is the error message and the second optional parameter can be one of the values for the PHP function `trigger_error()`. The default value of the level parameter is E_USER_WARNING.

display

```
void display ( string template [, string cache_id [, string compile_id]])
```

This method displays the template. The first parameter is the template name with or without the resource type and path. The second optional parameter is `cache_id` for multiple caches and the third optional parameter is `compile_id`.

fetch

```
string fetch ( string template [, string cache_id [, string compile_id [,
bool display ]]])
```

This method returns the output of a template or displays the template. It has the same parameters as the display method with one optional parameter more, the `display` Boolean parameter, which is `false` by default. If it is set to `true`, the effect of this method will be the same as the `display()` method.

The `display()` method is built like this:

```
function display($resource_name, $cache_id = null, $compile_id = null)
    {
        $this->fetch($resource_name, $cache_id, $compile_id, true);
    }
```

Therefore, you should use the `display()` method when you want to display a template and the `fetch()` method when you want to get the output of a template.

config_load

```
void config_load ( string file [, string section])
```

This method loads the configuration file data and assigns it to the template. The first parameter is the name of the configuration file and the second optional parameter is the section of the configuration file we need to load.

get_registered_object

```
array get_registered_object ( string object_name)
```

This method returns a reference to a registered object. The parameter is the registered object's name.

clear_config

```
void clear_config ( [string var])
```

This method clears all assigned configuration variables if no parameter is provided. If the optional var parameter is specified it will clear only that configuration variable.

Summary

In this chapter, we looked at Smarty from the programmer's point of view. We saw the many built-in Smarty variables as well as methods that make the programmer's job easy. You can use the methods and variables covered to perform various functions ranging from caching to debugging to registering filters.

9
Caching and Performance

Caching is a technique that is used very frequently by programmers to avoid calculating or generating the same output repeatedly. Instead, function results or even output are recorded and saved for later reuse. Usually caching is done by saving the appropriate information in special files on disk, and then retrieving it later, but you could just as well cache things in memory.

A simple way to introduce caching to your PHP scripts is by using the `static` keyword for a variable on functions, and using that variable to keep an in-memory copy of the function results, such as in the following code snippet:

```php
<?php
function getUserID($username)
{
    global $conn;
    static $returns;

    // check if we already have the result of
    // this function for the given username
    if (!empty($returns[$username])) {
        return $returns[$username];
    }

    $stmt = "SELECT
                user_id
             FROM
                user
             WHERE
                user_name='" . addslashes($username) . "'";
    $result = mysql_query($stmt, $conn);
    if ($result) {
        $user_id = mysql_result($result, 0, 0);
        // cache this result for later
        $returns[$username] = $user_id;
        return $user_id;
    }
}

// first call will trigger a DB query
$user_id = getUserID('andrei');
// second call will get its results from the cache
$user_id = getUserID('andrei');
?>
```

That is a nice example of an in-memory cache system (although extremely simple), but that's not how Smarty caches templates. Smarty caches the templates files into other files, where the actual output is saved and reused later if caching is enabled. Let's go over how to use this very handy feature.

Caching in Smarty

By default, a Smarty template has caching disabled (as of version 2.6.10), but you can always enable it manually on your PHP scripts by setting the caching property to 1, as in:

```php
<?php
include_once('libs/Smarty.class.php');
$smarty = new Smarty;
$smarty->caching = 1;

$smarty->display('example2.tpl');
?>
```

This will speed things up by saving the output of a template file into a cache file, and using that file in the future, instead of regenerating the output again from scratch. In some cases, the speed gain as a result of this feature is dramatic. The lifetime of each cached file defaults to one hour from its creation.

You need to be aware of what this means for your particular application, since this type of caching may not be suitable for everything. That is, refreshing your cached files every hour might be too long for your particular case, or maybe even too short. The lifetime can be tweaked on a per-cached-file basis, by setting the caching property to 2, and then changing the cache_lifetime property as you wish. Here's an example:

```php
<?php
include_once('libs/Smarty.class.php');
$smarty = new Smarty;

// set the lifetime per cached file
$smarty->caching = 2;

// set the lifetime for 2 hours
$smarty->cache_lifetime = 7200;
$smarty->display('example3.tpl');

// set the lifetime for 1 day
$smarty->cache_lifetime = 24 * 60 * 60;
$smarty->display('daily_favorites.tpl');
?>
```

In the example above, we set the cache lifetime of the example3.tpl template file to two hours, and set the lifetime to one day for the daily_favorites.tpl template. As you can guess from the name, the template file doesn't need to be generated that frequently, since it is simply displaying the previous day's favorite links. As mentioned before, the best way to improve the performance of PHP scripts is to spend some time analyzing your application. See if tweaking the cache lifetime for each particular template will make sense or not.

While these features are extremely useful in some situations, you might want to automatically refresh the cache if a template file was updated. Smarty's compile_check property allows you to do just that, since it forces the template engine to check whether any template or config files associated with this cache have been updated, and if so, regenerates the cache. In order to enable this feature, just set this property to TRUE, as in:

```php
<?php
include_once('smarty.class.php');
$smarty = new smarty;
$smarty->caching = 1;
$smarty->compile_check = TRUE;

$smarty->display('example4.tpl');
?>
```

Of course, enabling this feature will affect performance, since Smarty will need to check all the associated files for their modified dates.

Dynamically Caching Template Sections

Smarty's caching features are very interesting, but the options outlined above are still pretty inflexible. Another interesting feature is the ability to check whether a given template is already cached or not with the is_cached function. This is important because it allows the programmer to only execute code when strictly necessary. For instance, you could decide whether to run an expensive database query or not based on whether the given template is still available on Smarty's cache. The following example illustrates this feature:

```php
<?php
include_once('libs/smarty.class.php');
$smarty = new Smarty;
$smarty->caching = 1;

// only run this SQL query if necessary
if (!$smarty->is_cached('templates/example4.tpl')) {
    $stmt = "SELECT
                user_id,
                user_full_name
            FROM
                user
            WHERE
                user_name='" . addslashes($username) . "'";
    $result = mysql_query($stmt, $conn);
    if ($result) {
        $row = mysql_fetch_assoc($result);
        $smarty->assign('user_info', $row);
    }
}

$smarty->display('example4.tpl');
?>
```

As you can see, the is_cached() function expects a template filename as the first argument and will return TRUE if the given template is found in the cache.

Clearing the Cache

You can clear out individual template files with the clear_cache() function and also the whole cache with clear_all_cache. While usually you would wait for Smarty to automatically clear the cached version of a template by making use of the lifetime feature, you can also manually trigger this procedure. Here's an example of how you can clear the cache for a specific template file:

```php
<?php
include_once('libs/smarty.class.php');
$smarty = new smarty;
$smarty->caching = 1;

// remove the cache for this particular template
$smarty->clear_cache('templates/example6.tpl');

$smarty->display('example6.tpl');
?>
```

The following is an example of how to completely clear Smarty's cache:

```php
<?php
include_once('libs/smarty.class.php');
$smarty = new smarty;
$smarty->caching = 1;

// fully clear the Smarty cache
$smarty->clear_all_cache();

$smarty->display('example7.tpl');
?>
```

One thing that is very important to remember is that Smarty will not automatically remove the cache files that are older than their configured lifetime. That is, if you set a specific template to expire after two hours, the file will continue to exist until some PHP script removes it, or the template needs to be re-generated. Therefore, it's always a good idea to build a quick PHP script to remove cache files to save disk space. You can do that with an optional argument to the clear_all_cache() function to hold the number of seconds since the cache file was created, like so:

```php
<?php
include_once('libs/smarty.class.php');
$smarty = new smarty;
$smarty->caching = 1;
$smarty->compile_check = true;

// expiration is 2 hours
$expiration_secs = 2 * 60 * 60;
$smarty->clear_all_cache($expiration_secs);
?>
```

Advanced Caching Features

While it may seem that the caching features outlined so far are very useful (and they are!), they will quickly fall short for a semi-complex website. Take for example, a portal-like website with sections like news, weblogs, and photos. You may want to cache the output of all specific news items, and re-generate them in 5 days. On this specific case, the existing caching functionality will not be enough, as the cache is associated with a template file, but this template file is re-used for all news items.

The feature that is available and overcomes this apparent lack of functionality is the ability to create multiple caches per template file. You do that by passing a second parameter to the display method, which Smarty will use that to create a sub-directory under the cache directory to hold the cache files. Take the following PHP script as an example:

```php
<?php
include_once('libs/smarty.class.php');
$smarty = new Smarty;
$smarty->caching = 1;

// $_GET['id'] holds the integer 8143
$news_entry_id = (integer) $_GET['id'];
if (!$smarty->is_cached('news.tpl', $news_entry_id)) {
    $info = get_news_article_details($news_entry_id);
    $smarty->assign(array(
        'news_entry_id'    => $info['news_id'],
        'news_entry_title' => $info['news_title']
    ));
}

$smarty->display('news.tpl', $news_entry_id);
?>
```

By default, Smarty will create all cache files in a directory named cache under the current working directory. Running the example above will result in a file being created, with a filename similar to news^8143^%%A9^A9B^A9B6E5C0%%news.tpl.

A problem with that scenario is that for complicated websites with lots of cached content, all of the cached files will be located at the same directory, which will slow down access on most operating systems.

Using Cache Groups

It's a good thing that the Smarty developers have already thought about this problem, and provided yet another feature to customize how the cache files are stored. Consider the following modified script:

```php
<?php
include_once('libs/smarty.class.php');
$smarty = new smarty;
$smarty->caching = 1;
$smarty->use_sub_dirs = TRUE;

// $_GET['id'] holds the integer 8143
$news_entry_id = (integer) $_GET['id'];
if (!$smarty->is_cached('news.tpl', 'news|'.$news_entry_id)) {
    $info = get_news_article_details($news_entry_id);
    $smarty->assign(array(
        'news_entry_id'    => $info['news_id'],
        'news_entry_title' => $info['news_title']
    ));
}

$smarty->display('news.tpl', 'news|'.$news_entry_id);
?>
```

By setting the use_sub_dirs property to TRUE, and using a special format while creating the cache ID, we cause Smarty to create the following directory structure to store the cache file:

cache\news\8143\%%A9\A9B\A9B6E5C0%%news.tpl

As you can see, Smarty created a sub-directory called news inside the cache directory, and yet another sub-directory called 8143 under it. The other sub-directories, and the file-name format are internal details for Smarty, but the important thing here is that by grouping cache IDs with the pipe character, you can control how cache files are stored and removed.

Clearing a Cache Group

This may seem simple, but think about a medium size website with hundreds or even thousands of different news pieces. If all of the cached files were stored on a single directory, code that needs to touch these files would be significantly slower than desired. If there are thousands of different news pieces, you could remove them all at once with a simple PHP script, like so:

```php
<?php
include_once('smarty.class.php');
$smarty = new smarty;
$smarty->template_dir = 'templates/';
$smarty->caching = 1;
$smarty->use_sub_dirs = TRUE;

$smarty->clear_cache(null, 'news');
?>
```

The clear_cache function goes to the cache directory, and simply removes the whole news sub-directory tree: all sub-directories and files contained within it. The good thing here is that you don't have to remove your complete cache if you simply want to change something on the news section of your website.

Similar to how you can conditionally clear cache files by passing the number of seconds since the cache file was created, you may do the same thing with a cache group. The following is an example that will remove all cache files within the news group that are older than an hour:

```php
<?php
include_once('smarty.class.php');
$smarty = new smarty;
$smarty->template_dir = 'templates/';
$smarty->caching = 1;
$smarty->use_sub_dirs = TRUE;

// expiration is 1 hour
$expiration_secs = 1 * 60 * 60;
$smarty->clear_cache(null, 'news', null, $expiration_secs);
?>
```

The third argument needs to be set to null, and Smarty will take care of the rest. The example above is a great candidate of a potential PHP script to be run from a *crontab*, so that the cache files get removed every hour or so.

Avoiding the Cache

There might be some specific cases in which you don't want Smarty to cache the template output, or even small portions of a particular template. In these cases, you have several options to avoid the cache:

- Force a specific template not to be cached.
- Always use {insert} when you need dynamic content, since it doesn't use the caching system.
- Create a custom plug-in to force Smarty not to cache certain portions of a template.

We will go over these three different methods next.

Disabling a Template Cache

As already discussed, you can disable Smarty's cache feature on a template level by simply setting the `caching` property to 0 (zero):

```php
<?php
include_once('smarty.class.php');
$smarty = new smarty;
$smarty->caching = 0;

$smarty->display('example4.tpl');
?>
```

Using {insert} to Avoid Caching

You could also bypass Smarty's cache system by using the `{insert}` function, and implementing a custom PHP function to return the appropriate results. For instance, you might want to have a highly dynamic portion of your site to display the current time at each user location. The caching feature will be a problem in this specific case, so let's consider the following PHP script:

```php
<?php
include_once('smarty.class.php');
$smarty = new smarty;
$smarty->template_dir = 'templates/';
$smarty->caching = 1;
$smarty->use_sub_dirs = TRUE;

if (!$smarty->is_cached('example12.tpl')) {
    $smarty->assign('name', 'Joao Prado Maia');
}

$smarty->display('example12.tpl');
?>
```

As you can see, we are conditionally setting the `name` template variable depending on whether the template is already cached or not. Let's see how the actual template is laid out:

```html
<html>
<head>
    <title>Untitled</title>
</head>
<body>
<p>Hello {$name}</p>
{insert name="get_local_time" city="houston"}
</body>
</html>
```

We will require a new file in Smarty's plug-in directory called `insert.get_local_time.php`. Here's the source code for this file:

```php
<?php
// let's re-use PEAR's Date package for this function
require_once('Date.php');

function smarty_insert_get_local_time($params, &$smarty)
{
    if ($params['city'] == 'houston') {
        $date = new Date();
        // convert to the CST timezone
        $date->convertTZByID('America/Chicago');
        // getDate() returns the date formatted on the following format:
        // i.e. 2005-12-21 12:34:32
        $local_time = $date->getDate();
    }
```

```
    // ... continue with other cities
    return $local_time;
}
?>
```

By opening this PHP script on your web browser, you should see something similar to the following:

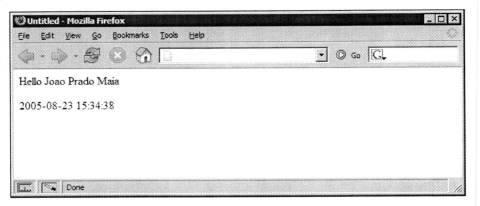

Now try going back to the front-end PHP script, and changing the name template variable to something else, then reloading your web browser. You will realize that the name is not changing on the page, but the local time is.

Creating a Custom Plug-in to Avoid Caching on Portions of a Template

The last method of avoiding the cache system is pretty straightforward. All we need to do is to create a custom block plug-in, and register it with Smarty as a non-cacheable one. This way when Smarty needs to process a particular portion of a template enclosed by our plug-in, the content will always be dynamic.

This is also convenient because it gives a lot of control to the template programmer, while avoiding the need for a custom {insert} function each time you need some truly dynamic content. Let's analyze an implementation of this method:

```php
<?php
include_once('libs/smarty.class.php');
$smarty = new smarty();
$smarty->caching = 1;
$smarty->use_sub_dirs = TRUE;
function get_content($params, $content, &$smarty)
{
return $content;
}
$smarty->register_block('no_caching', 'get_content', false);
if (!$smarty->is_cached('example13.tpl')) {
    $smarty->assign('name', 'Joao Prado Maia');
}
// we want to always display the most up to date download stats
$smarty->assign('download_stats', 1200);
$smarty->display('example13.tpl');
?>
```

What the custom plug-in is doing is very simple—it's being registered as a non-cacheable Smarty plug-in, and returning the content found within the {no_caching} tags.

This is what the output of this template looks like within a web browser:

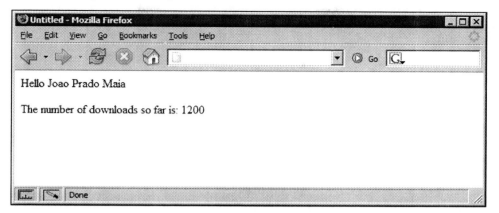

In order to test this feature, try changing both the `name` and `download_stats` variables to something else, and see which one actually gets changed when looking from your web browser. You will see that the `name` variable keeps the old value, and `download_stats` is truly dynamic.

Creating a Custom Cache Handler

While Smarty's caching system works extremely well for small to medium-sized websites, it will eventually pose a problem for bigger portals. Consider the scenario of a semi-complex website that is handled by several servers. Let's assume this portal is managed over multiple web servers to balance the load in a simple round-robin fashion across several machines, and there is a central database server that is used to store the website's content.

Now continue with this scenario and imagine these web servers, each keeping a different cache copy of a particular template. What would happen if a particular section of the site was changed, and the cached copy on the first web server was updated, but the one on the second server wasn't? There is a wide range of potential problems that could happen here, and an advanced feature is needed to fill this gap.

Smarty's answer to this problem is the ability to provide a custom cache handler function to manage the caching system content. The easiest answer to the problem scenario described above would be to write a custom cache handler, and save the cache content on the central database server. That way, all of the different web servers will transparently connect to the database to get content, and if something changes on a cached template, all web servers are updated at once.

In order to create this custom cache handler backed by a database we will need to:

- Create a separate database to host this cached content (optional).
- Create a table to hold this content.
- Build a PHP function to handle the caching and store the content on the database.
- Point Smarty to this PHP function so it knows that it needs to call it to write or read cached content.

Let's go over each of those steps now, starting with the database setup. The first thing needed here is to connect to the MySQL database server and create a new database, which we will call cache:

```
$ mysql -u root -p
Enter password: ******
Welcome to the MySQL monitor.  Commands end with ; or \g.
Your MySQL connection id is 12 to server version: 4.1.14-max-debug

Type 'help;' or '\h' for help. Type '\c' to clear the buffer.

mysql> CREATE DATABASE cache;
Query OK, 1 row affected (0.00 sec)

mysql> USE cache;
Database changed

mysql> CREATE TABLE smarty_cache (
    ->     id INT(11) UNSIGNED NOT NULL AUTO_INCREMENT,
    ->     template_file VARCHAR(32) NOT NULL,
    ->     cache_id VARCHAR(32) DEFAULT NULL,
    ->     compile_id VARCHAR(32) DEFAULT NULL,
    ->     contents MEDIUMTEXT NOT NULL,
    ->     PRIMARY KEY (id)
    -> );
Query OK, 0 rows affected (0.00 sec)

mysql> GRANT SELECT, UPDATE, INSERT, DELETE ON cache.* TO 'cache_user'@'localhost'
IDENTIFIED BY '4Ef6Th23qw';
Query OK, 0 rows affected (0.00 sec)
```

The first command creates the new database called cache that we will use, the second one changes the currently selected database to this newly created one, and then we create the smarty_cache table. The last command grants the appropriate permissions to a new MySQL user called cache_user. This new user requires the permission to run UPDATE, DELETE, INSERT and SELECT statements against this database.

Now that the database is all set up for us, let's start building the actual custom cache handler function. The following are the required function arguments for any cache handler in Smarty:

Argument	Description
$action	The action that Smarty is trying to perform on the cache. Possible values are: write, read, or clear. That is, write to the cache, read from the cache, or clear the contents of the cache for a particular template.
&$smarty	The Smarty object that is currently processing this template. This might be useful for caching systems that need to have access to some internal-only detail of the template file, or from Smarty itself. This is always passed as a reference, so it is also available to be modified from the cache handler.
&$cache_contents	The variable that will hold the contents to be put in the cache, or to be written to in the case of a read action, or even a dummy value in the case of a clear action. This variable is passed as a reference, and should be set to whatever is available on the cache in the case of a read action.
$template_file	The filename of the template file that this cache should relate to.
$cache_id	(Optional.) The cache group with which to associate this cache.

Argument	Description
$compile_id	(Optional.) The compile ID with which to associate this cache.
$expiration_time	(Optional.) The expiration time for this particular cache item. This is strictly optional since Smarty already checks the expiration time prior to calling the cache system, but it could be used for some extra processing by the cache handler itself.

We will call this cache handler function db_cache_handler, and store the function in the file db_cache_handler.php and re-use it in the actual PHP scripts. Here's the start of this file:

```php
<?php
require_once('DB.php');
// connect to the database server
$dsn = array(
    'phptype'  => 'mysql',
    'hostspec' => 'localhost',
    'username' => 'cache_user',
    'password' => '4Ef6Th23qw',
    'database' => 'cache'
);
$dbh = DB::connect($dsn);
```

The above will include the PEAR::DB package, which is usually installed by default on most modern PHP installations, assign the proper values to the connection DSN variable, and then connect to the database server. Next we will define the actual PHP function:

```php
function db_cache_handler($action, &$smarty, &$cache_contents,
        $template_file = null, $cache_id = null,
        $compile_id = null, $expiration_time = null)
{
    global $dbh;
```

That defines a new function called db_cache_handler, and uses the argument list described before. We also define a $dbh global variable to be able to access the database connection handle and use it from within the PHP function.

```php
// build the where clause
$where_params = array();
if (!empty($template_file)) {
    $where_params[] = "template_file='" . addslashes($template_file) . "'";
}
if (!empty($cache_id)) {
    $where_params[] = "cache_id='" . addslashes($cache_id) . "'";
}
if (!empty($compile_id)) {
    $where_params[] = "compile_id='" . addslashes($compile_id) . "'";
}
$where_clause = implode(' AND ', $where_params);
```

The above will dynamically build an array with the function arguments, to eventually re-use in the SQL queries themselves. Now we go over each possible action type:

```php
// possible values for $action are: read, write or clear
if ($action == 'read') {
    $stmt = "SELECT
                contents
            FROM
                smarty_cache
            WHERE " . $where_clause;
    $cache_contents = $dbh->getOne($stmt);
```

As you can see, the read action will trigger a SELECT query against the database to get the actual cache content, and it will assign it to the $cache_contents variable, which is passed by reference to this function. This will allow the PHP code that calls this function to access the contents at will.

```php
} elseif ($action == 'write') {
    // check if this is already cached
    $stmt = "SELECT
                id
            FROM
                smarty_cache
            WHERE " . $where_clause;
    $id = $dbh->getOne($stmt);
    if (empty($id)) {
        $stmt = "INSERT INTO
                    smarty_cache
                (
                    template_file,
                    cache_id,
                    compile_id,
                    contents
                ) VALUES (
                    '" . addslashes($template_file) . "',
                    '" . addslashes($cache_id) . "',
                    '" . addslashes($compile_id) . "',
                    '" . addslashes($cache_contents) . "'
                )";
    } else {
        $stmt = "UPDATE
                    smarty_cache
                SET
                    template_file='" . addslashes($template_file) . "',
                    cache_id='" . addslashes($cache_id) . "',
                    compile_id='" . addslashes($compile_id) . "',
                    contents='" . addslashes($cache_contents) . "'
                WHERE
                    id=$id";
    }
    $dbh->query($stmt);
```

The code above is simply checking if the given template is already in the cache, and if it is, it will run an UPDATE query against it. Otherwise, it will insert the new template. The rest of the script will handle the last clear action, which is used to delete a particular cache entry from the database:

```php
} elseif ($action == 'clear') {
    $stmt = "DELETE FROM
                smarty_cache
            WHERE " . $where_clause;
    $dbh->query($stmt);
}
}
?>
```

You should concatenate the previous PHP snippets together into the db_cache_handler.php file, and save it. Next we will finish the cache handler example with the actual PHP script:

```php
<?php
include_once('libs/smarty.class.php');
include_once('db_cache_handler.php');
$smarty = new Smarty;
$smarty->caching = 1;
$smarty->compile_check = false;
$smarty->cache_handler_func = 'db_cache_handler';
```

```
if (!$smarty->is_cached('cache_handler.tpl')) {
    $smarty->assign('name', 'Joao Prado Maia');
}

$smarty->display('cache_handler.tpl');
?>
```

The cache_handler_func Smarty property is what tells the template engine to use our custom PHP script as the source for all things related to the cache system. Smarty will call that function when it needs to check if a template is already cached, like the is_cached check above, or when trying to save a new version of a cached template, and so on. Here's the source code for the accompanying cache_handler.tpl template file:

```
<html>
<head>
    <title>Custom Cache Handler Example</title>
</head>

<body>

<p>Hello {$name}</p>

</body>
</html>
```

While the template is extremely simple—it only tries to print the given $name variable—it will be a perfect example for us to test our custom cache handler. Try loading the PHP script on your browser, and you see this simple web page:

Nothing fancy about that. Let's go a little deeper and actually see what is being stored on the database itself:

```
$ mysql -u root -p cache
Enter password: ******
Welcome to the MySQL monitor.  Commands end with ; or \g.
Your MySQL connection id is 26 to server version: 4.1.14-max-debug

Type 'help;' or '\h' for help. Type '\c' to clear the buffer.

mysql> SELECT * FROM smarty_cache\G
*************************** 1. row ***************************
        id: 1
```

```
template_file: cache_handler.tpl
     cache_id:
   compile_id:
     contents: 139
a:4:{s:8:"template";a:1:{s:17:"cache_handler.tpl";b:1;}s:9:"timestamp";i:1125464
354;s:7:"expires";i:1125467954;s:13:"cache_serials";a:0:{}}<html>
<head>
        <title>Custom Cache Handler Example</title>
</head>

<body>

<p>Hello Joao Prado Maia</p>

</body>
</html>
1 row in set (0.27 sec)
```

As you can see, the actual cache contents have a specific format to them, which is used by Smarty to find extra information about each particular cache entry. The real format doesn't really matter, as Smarty will give you the value already pre-formatted for you.

Optimizing Smarty Applications

While caching in most cases will provide a big boost of performance, it isn't the only way to performance-tune your PHP / Smarty applications. Usually web applications will need to be analyzed carefully to find performance-related problems. Sometimes they might be related to your database server, if you use one, or even depend on an algorithm that you decided to use for a particular task. Doing a complete analysis of your application might need the help of other people, who are new to your code and can look at it with a fresh perspective.

Here are some simple guidelines that might help you get a performance-centric view of developing with PHP and Smarty:

- Implement periodic performance tests on your code.
- Document the results of your performance tests.
- Use profiler tools such as Xdebug and CacheGrind.
- Consider a PHP optimizer solution, such as ionCube's PHP Accelerator or Zend Optimizer.
- Enable the caching feature in Smarty.
- Implement caching routines on your back-end PHP code.
- Precompute function results when appropriate.
- Stay current with PHP releases, as new versions frequently include performance enhancements.

From all of the above items, the first two ones are the most important. Without periodic tests, and a plan to always document the results, there is no way to tell which part of the code is performing poorly. At the same time, when testing improvements to the code, try to make changes in only one area of the code, and then perform the tests again. Large changes to the code will sometimes affect the testing results in different ways.

Profiling PHP

One of PHP's historical problems is the lack of good tools aimed at profiling and debugging. Since the language was created, most programmers have been taught to simply add profiling lines through the PHP code to be able to see in which part the script is actually taking the most time in. The following script would be a good example of the old way of doing things:

```php
<?php
include_once('Benchmark/Timer.php');
$bench = new Benchmark_Timer;
$bench->start();

include_once('smarty.class.php');
$smarty = new smarty;
$smarty->caching = 0;
$bench->setMarker(__LINE__);

// fully clear the Smarty cache
$smarty->assign('name', 'Joao Prado Maia');

$smarty->display('cache_handler.tpl');

$bench->stop();
var_dump($bench->getProfiling());
?>
```

The script is reusing an existing benchmarking utility from PEAR called Benchmark_Timer, and will display an array that contains the benchmarking information, which is built by repeatedly calling the benchmark code that computes the current timestamp and the difference to the previous call, hence calculating the difference in time from one part of the code to the next. Here's what this script would output on your browser:

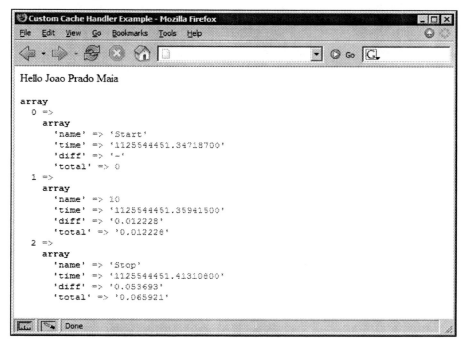

The information displayed on the screenshot above is pretty useful, but profiling PHP scripts this way is extremely error prone and laborious, since you need to take the time to add the benchmark class to your application, and sprinkle your code with calls to the appropriate function.

Fortunately, there's a better way to profile PHP scripts with some fairly recent open-source tools. We will go over some of them next.

Designing Sites for Effective Caching

One of the most important things while designing a new website or application is to think of how the user will eventually access your information. One of the corner stones of the Web is the use of proxy servers that cache things for the end user, usually done by Internet Service Providers (ISP) to improve the user experience of the Web. Web browsers also cache things locally to improve the speed of frequently accessed websites.

This is done by using four different HTTP headers that will command how the proxy servers and web browsers cache content:

- Last-Modified
- ETag
- Expires
- Cache-Control

We will go over these headers next, and how to manipulate them to improve the caching of your website or application.

The Last-Modified and ETag Headers

Most web servers nowadays return valid content automatically for these two headers, which are used by user agents (web browsers and proxy servers) to check whether a given URL should be cached or not. The following would be a good example of a HTTP response that includes these two headers:

```
HTTP/1.1 200 OK
Date: Thu, 29 Sep 2005 18:54:26 GMT
Server: Apache/1.3.33 (Unix)
Cache-Control: max-age=3600, must-revalidate
Expires: Sat, 29 Oct 2005 18:54:26 GMT
Last-Modified: Thu, 29 Sep 2005 18:54:26 GMT
ETag: "6e93-130-3852bdde"
Content-Length: 3489
Content-Type: text/html
```

The Last-Modified header is used to tell the user agent when this content was generated and it will be re-used later when the user agent needs to check whether the server has a fresher version of the content than the one it has cached locally. This check is done by yet another HTTP header, called If-Modified-Since, which will be passed to the server, and will help decide whether the local cache should be used or not. Here's a simple example:

```
GET /cnn/images/1.gif HTTP/1.1
Host: i.cnn.net
Accept: image/png,*/*;q=0.5
```

```
Accept-Language: en-us,en;q=0.5
Accept-Encoding: gzip,deflate
Accept-Charset: ISO-8859-1,utf-8;q=0.7,*;q=0.7
If-Modified-Since: Tue, 27 May 2003 19:00:10 GMT
Cache-Control: max-age=0
```

As you can see above, the 1.gif image was probably previously returned with a Last-Modified value of Tue, 27 May 2003 19:00:10 GMT, and that value is being sent back to the server to see whether the web browser should use the local cached copy of this image, or if it should request a new copy. Here's the response from the server:

```
HTTP/1.x 304 Not Modified
Date: Sat, 03 Sep 2005 04:15:42 GMT
Content-Type: image/gif
Last-Modified: Tue, 27 May 2003 19:00:10 GMT
Age: 987
Connection: keep-alive
```

The 304 response code is what tells the web browser to simply re-use the local cached copy.

The ETag header is used in a similar way to the Last-Modified one, but this time a unique identifier created by the server that relates to that specific version of the content. Here's an example HTTP request:

```
GET /cnn/.element/img/1.3/searchbar/bg.gif HTTP/1.1
Host: i.a.cnn.net
Accept: image/png,*/*;q=0.5
Accept-Language: en-us,en;q=0.5
Accept-Encoding: gzip,deflate
Accept-Charset: ISO-8859-1,utf-8;q=0.7,*;q=0.7
If-Modified-Since: Wed, 09 Mar 2005 17:32:07 GMT
If-None-Match: "d0b3114c-1b1-9b-0"
Cache-Control: max-age=0
```

The If-None-Match header value above is what is passed by the user agent to the server, to check whether the local cached copy of this image is still valid or not. If it is, the web server will return a 304 response code as it did for the If-Modified-Since example we described before:

```
HTTP/1.x 304 Not Modified
Content-Type: image/gif
Last-Modified: Wed, 09 Mar 2005 17:32:07 GMT
Etag: "d0b3114c-182-9b-0"
Date: Sat, 03 Sep 2005 04:44:30 GMT
Connection: close
```

As you can see, the server will return the 304 response code, and the same ETag value, to demonstrate to the user agent that its local copy is still valid and it should be used.

The Expires Header

This header allows you to set an expiration date for a particular piece of content on your website or application. It is most useful for static content, such as images for buttons and logos. Since these things don't tend to change very often, you can set a very long expiration date on them, and it will improve the performance of your pages since some of their content will be delivered through caches.

The allowed value for this header is an HTTP date set to Greenwich Mean Time (GMT). That alone brings a potential problem, since depending on how synchronized the clocks on your web server and the cache user agent are, you might get stale content that is deemed fresh. Here's an example of the use of the Expires header:

```
HTTP/1.x 200 OK
Date: Sat, 03 Sep 2005 05:06:24 GMT
Server: Apache
Content-Type: text/html
Last-Modified: Sat, 03 Sep 2005 05:06:17 GMT
Cache-Control: max-age=60, private
Expires: Sat, 03 Dec 2005 05:06:24 GMT
Content-Encoding: gzip
Content-Length: 13606
Connection: close
```

As you can see above, the Expires header is being set to 3 months in the future, which is just fine in this specific case since it is the response for a navigation bar image that doesn't get changed very often, if at all.

The Cache-Control Header

This header was introduced with HTTP 1.1 to provide more control to proxy servers and overall cache maintenance. There are several values that can be used for this response header:

Header Value	Description
max-age=[seconds]	Amount of time for which the cached content will be deemed valid.
s-maxage=[seconds]	Same as above header value, but only appropriate to proxy caches.
public	Flags authenticated responses as cacheable.
no-cache	Instructs caches to submit the request to the web server before releasing any content. Useful in combination with authenticated requests.
no-store	Prevents caches from storing any content.
must-revalidate	Forces caches to obey your expiration rules.
proxy-revalidate	Similar to must-revalidate, but specific to proxy caches.

Here's an example of how to mark a specific URL as being cacheable, but still force caches to check with the web server before releasing any content:

```
Cache-Control: public, no-cache, must-revalidate
```

Tools: ApacheBench (ab)

ApacheBench is a simple benchmarking tool that comes bundled with most Apache HTTP Server distributions, so if you already have this web server installed, it's safe to say that you also have ApacheBench. The command that you should look for is called ab.

We will not go over many details about it, but here's a simple example of how to use this tool to benchmark a specific web page:

```
$ ab -n 100 -c 10 http://pessoal.org/blog/index.php
```

If you need to provide authentication credentials to connect to this web page, you may pass them along with ab:

```
$ ab -n 100 -c 10 -A username:password http://pessoal.org/blog/index.php
```

There are several different options that you can use with this tool, so run it with the –h argument to see an overview of them. Here's a sample output (given that you provide the proper URL to it):

```
This is ApacheBench, Version 2.0.41-dev <$Revision: 1.121.2.12 $> apache-2.0
Copyright (c) 1996 Adam Twiss, Zeus Technology Ltd, http://www.zeustech.net/
Copyright (c) 1998-2002 The Apache Software Foundation, http://www.apache.org/

Benchmarking pessoal.org (be patient).....done


Server Software:        Apache/2.0.46
Server Hostname:        pessoal.org
Server Port:            80

Document Path:          /blog/index.php
Document Length:        19194 bytes

Concurrency Level:      10
Time taken for tests:   8.263694 seconds
Complete requests:      100
Failed requests:        0
Write errors:           0
Total transferred:      1947100 bytes
HTML transferred:       1919400 bytes
Requests per second:    12.10 [#/sec] (mean)
Time per request:       826.369 [ms] (mean)
Time per request:       82.637 [ms] (mean, across all concurrent requests)
Transfer rate:          230.04 [Kbytes/sec] received

Connection Times (ms)
              min  mean[+/-sd] median   max
Connect:       51    56   9.3     52      87
Processing:   359   752 259.8    711    1526
Waiting:      173   474 214.0    443    1195
Total:        419   808 258.6    767    1577

Percentage of the requests served within a certain time (ms)
  50%    767
  66%    833
  75%    905
  80%   1037
  90%   1198
  95%   1328
  98%   1535
  99%   1577
 100%   1577 (longest request)
```

From the output above, we can gather that the web page averaged 12 requests per second, with an average of 82.63 milliseconds taken per request.

Tools: Xdebug

Xdebug is a Zend extension that provides a lot of useful debugging and profiling information to PHP developers. This tool is maintained by Derick Rethans, who is a core PHP developer and an active member of the community. We will cover the 2.0 branch of this tool, as it provides some very interesting features, one of them being the integration with CacheGrind, which allows PHP developers to analyze profile information with a graphical tool.

Xdebug can be downloaded from its website at http://www.xdebug.org. Look for the download link that is associated with the 2.0 branch, usually a URL that begins with xdebug200.

We will go over the installation instructions for Windows users, assuming an Apache installation with PHP set up as a module. The process is pretty simple, as the download link will provide you with a ready-to-use DLL file. The file for our instructions will be called xdebug-5.0-2.0.0beta1.dll. Here is the step-by-step process:

1. Copy the DLL file to the PHP extensions directory, which is usually c:\php\ext.

2. Open your php.ini file (stored on c:\windows).

3. Add the following lines to the beginning of the file (right after the [PHP] line):
   ```
   zend_extension_ts="c:/php/ext/xdebug-5.0-2.0.0beta1.dll"
   xdebug.profiler_enable=1
   xdebug.profiler_output_dir="c:/tmp/xdebug/"
   ```

4. Restart Apache.

5. Load a web page from a domain hosted on this web server.

The first of the three lines that you added to php.ini will tell PHP to load the Xdebug extension while processing PHP scripts and the other two lines are needed by Xdebug to enable the features that will generate dump files to be used when analyzing the profile information of your page.

Please make sure to provide the proper permissions on the c:\tmp\xdebug directory so that the Apache server is allowed to create files within it.

Now take a look at the c:\tmp\xdebug directory. It should look somewhat like the following figure:

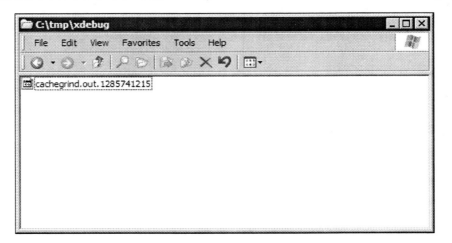

The files created within this directory will always conform to this cachegrind.out.<numbers> naming convention, and should be opened with WinCacheGrind, which we will describe next.

Tools: WinCacheGrind

WinCacheGrind is a graphical tool used to analyze the `cachegrind.out` files generated by Xdebug. This is an open-source project and you can download the latest release from its website at `http://sourceforge.net/projects/wincachegrind`.

Installation should be simple—just download the installer package and follow the step-by-step instructions. The tool should configure itself and work out of the box with the default options. After installing it, run the graphical tool itself.

From the main menu of WinCacheGrind, choose File, then Open. Browse through to `c:\tmp\xdebug` and open one of the `cachegrind.out` files. Your WinCacheGrind screen should look like the following:

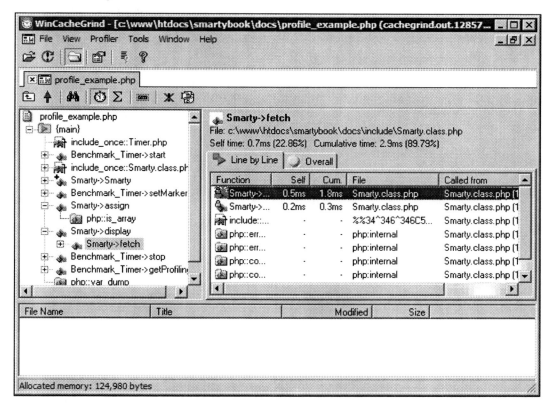

One of the most useful features is the ability to analyze the script execution as a whole, and see which function is using the largest portion of the time, and then drill down on that particular function and analyze its information. For relatively complex websites or applications, this can be crucial to tune the performance of some parts of your code that you don't expect are performance bottlenecks.

Summary

Performance is always a complex topic to discuss, and PHP is known for the lack of support from third-party tools in this respect. Hopefully, the growth of PHP's popularity will result in more work done to improve some of these tools.

Remember that performance tuning, and caching being one instrument towards that goal, should be considered on a case-by-case basis. Sometimes improving the performance of a piece of code will actually decrease the level of maintainability of the code, making it harder to understand and change in the future.

You should also understand and follow the guidelines to optimize Smarty applications. Specifically, the steps that describe the periodic performance tests and the documentation of the results of those tests are very important. Without an actual document describing the changes and the results, you will never be able to improve your code in the long term. Teams usually forget the changes previously done to an application, so always remember to document them.

10
Extending Smarty with Plug-ins

While Smarty was made to contain functions relevant to most common web development needs, there are times when you need to extend it. There are also some cases in which developing a Smarty plug-in is a good idea, because it might save you time or it might make sense to centralize a particular type of functionality into a single function call.

In this chapter, we will go over the process of finding, installing, and using plug-ins in templates, and also give an overview of how to implement your own custom functionality.

Smarty defines a plug-in as any type of custom functionality implemented by third-party developers. Smarty is already distributed with a wide variety of functions, and while some of them are needed by Smarty itself (called built-in functions), others can be changed to define some extra functionality (called custom functions). Plug-ins, however, are usually associated with totally different functionality not available by default in Smarty.

Finding and Installing Plug-ins

The best place to find plug-ins is by checking the resources listed on the Smarty website. At the time of writing this book, the biggest and most up-to-date collection of plug-ins can be found on the Smarty Wiki, available on `http://smarty.incutio.com/?page=smartyPlug-ins`. There's also a list of available plug-ins on the Smarty website, `http://smarty.php.net/resources.php`.

Installation of plug-ins should be as simple as moving the plug-in file into the appropriate location, usually the `plug-ins` directory under the Smarty installation path. For instance, if you installed Smarty under `/usr/local/share/Smarty`, you would need to copy your plug-in files to the `/usr/local/share/Smarty/plug-ins` directory. However, always refer to your plug-in documentation for the specific installation instructions.

Be aware of the naming convention for plug-ins—depending on the type of the plug-in, different filenames should be used. For example, for a modifier plug-in called `remove_whitespace`, you would need to create a file named `modifier.remove_whitespace.php` in your plug-ins directory.

Useful Plug-ins

In this section, we take a look at some handy plug-ins for Smarty.

HTML List Plug-in

While Smarty already provides a ton of useful functions to quickly generate HTML given a PHP array, it doesn't provide for a quick way to output lists (<OL> or <UL>). The HTML List plug-in is the answer to this deficiency, and it is available at http://smarty.incutio.com/ ?page=HTMLListPlugin. You need to copy the PHP code available on the URL and save it as function.html_list.php under the plugins directory.

In order to visually see the difference between using html_list and simply looping through a PHP array, here are two versions of a template that will generate the same output.

A PHP script, named example_html_list.php, to call out our template:

```php
<?php
include_once('libs/Smarty.class.php');
$smarty = new Smarty;

$departments = array(
    'Marketing Department',
    'Sales Department',
    'Customer Service Department'
);
$smarty->assign('departments', $departments);

$smarty->display('example_html_list.tpl');
?>
```

Looping through a PHP array with {section} in our example_html_list.tpl template file:

```
<html>
<head>
<title>Example Corp.</title>
</head>
<body>

Available departments:
<ul>
{section name="i" loop=$departments}
    <li>{$departments[i]}</li>
{/section}
</ul>

</body>
</html>
```

Using html_list instead:

```
<html>
<head>
<title>Example Corp.</title>
</head>
<body>

Available departments:
{html_list values=$departments}

</body>
</html>
```

And running this PHP script on your browser would result on the following output:

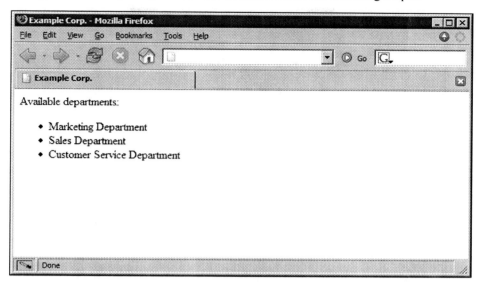

As you can see above, both ways of creating your template produce the same output, but the second form is much simpler to write and read, and because of that, it is easier to maintain.

File Size Format Plug-in

Web developers often need to quickly format a file size in bytes into a more human-readable format. While you could format the file size directly in PHP, and then pass that value to Smarty, you might want to use the original file size in bytes for something else. It's also a good idea to keep the business logic routines in PHP as simple as possible, and add layout logic to your Smarty templates later on.

This plug-in is available from `http://smarty.incutio.com/?page=FSizeFormatPlugin`. Check back often for updates to this plug-in.

The following is the source of `fsize_format`. Copy and save it as `modifier.fsize_format.php` in your plug-ins directory:

```php
<?php
/*
 * Smarty plugin
 * -------------------------------------------------------------
 * Type:     modifier
 * Name:     fsize_format
 * Version:  0.2
 * Date:     2003-05-15
 * Author:   Joscha Feth, joscha@feth.com
 * Purpose:  formats a filesize (in bytes) to human-readable format
 * Usage:    In the template, use
 *               {$filesize|fsize_format} => 123.45 B|KB|MB|GB|TB
 *           or
 *               {$filesize|fsize_format:"MB"} => 123.45 MB
 *           or
```

```
                        {$filesize|fsize_format:"TB":4} => 0.0012 TB
        * Params:
                        int     size            the filesize in bytes
                        string  format          the format, the output shall be: B, KB, MB,
        GB or TB
                        int     precision       the rounding precision
                        string  dec_point       the decimal separator
                        string  thousands_sep   the thousands separator
        * Install: Drop into the plugin directory
        * Version:
        *   2003-05-15  Version 0.2  - added dec_point and thousands_sep thanks to
        Thomas Brandl, tbrandl@barff.de
        *                            - made format always uppercase
        *                            - count sizes "on-the-fly"
        *   2003-02-21  Version 0.1  - initial release
        * ------------------------------------------------------------
        */
        function smarty_modifier_fsize_format($size,$format = '',$precision = 2,
        $dec_point = ".", $thousands_sep = ",")
        {
            $format = strtoupper($format);

            static $sizes = array();

            if (!count($sizes)) {
                $b = 1024;
                $sizes["B"] = 1;
                $sizes["KB"] = $sizes["B"] * $b;
                $sizes["MB"] = $sizes["KB"] * $b;
                $sizes["GB"] = $sizes["MB"] * $b;
                $sizes["TB"] = $sizes["GB"] * $b;
                $sizes = array_reverse($sizes, true);
            }

            // get "human" filesize
            foreach ($sizes as $unit => $bytes) {
                if (($size > $bytes) || ($unit == $format)) {
                    // return formatted size
                    return number_format($size / $bytes, $precision, $dec_point,
        $thousands_sep) . " " . $unit;
                }
            }
        }
        ?>
```

The code creates a PHP array with the definitions of each file size unit, such as a byte, kilobyte, megabyte, and so on. Then it reverses the order of those units, so the biggest ones are first. To finish it off, we loop through all of the available units, and see if the given file size is bigger than the unit being iterated on. So if you pass 1025 bytes as the file size, the code will loop through the units until it finds that 1025 is bigger than 1 kilobyte (1024 bytes). After finding the most appropriate unit, the code then formats the file size based on that unit.

Here's an example of the use of this plug-in:

The new PHP script named example_fsize_format.php to call out our template:

```
<?php
include_once('libs/Smarty.class.php');
$smarty = new Smarty;

// in real life you would do filesize('budget.pdf') here
$smarty->assign('filesize', 123456);

$smarty->display(example_fsize_format.tpl');
?>
```

And here is the `example_fsize_format.tpl` template file, with the call to the `fsize_format` variable modifier:

```
<html>
<head>
<title>Example Corp.</title>
</head>
<body>

Download file:
<ul>
  <li>
     <a href="download.php?file=budget.pdf">budget.pdf</a> (size:
{$filesize|fsize_format})
  </li>
</ul>

</body>
</html>
```

This is what the plug-in returns for the function call above: 120.56 KB.

As you can see from the documentation on this plug-in, you can even optionally force it to format the file size to a specific file size unit. Otherwise, the most appropriate unit will be used automatically by the plug-in.

Google Highlight Plug-in

A quite common problem in web development is to highlight the search keywords when displaying the results of a search. Google does this very well when one requests a cached copy of the web page that was returned by a search query, and this plug-in implements exactly this functionality. Perhaps the colors could be tweaked a little bit, but overall this is a very useful plug-in that can be relevant to your search engine results.

The following is the source code for our Google Highlight plug-in. Copy the source and paste into a new file called `modifier.google_highlight.php` in your plug-ins directory:

```
<?php
/*
 * Smarty plug-in
 * -------------------------------------------------------------
 * Type:     modifier
 * Name:     google_highlight
 * Version:  1.0
 * Date:     April 18, 2005
 * Author:   Jeroen de Jong <jeroen@telartis.nl>
 * Purpose:  html safe case insensitive google highlight
 * Comments: based on work by Tom Anderson <toma@etree.org>
 *
 * Example smarty code:
 *
{assign var=text value="This is a <a href=this>string</a> I want to search
through"}
{assign var=search value="this \"to search\" through"}
{$text|google_highlight:$search}
 *
 * -------------------------------------------------------------
 */
function smarty_modifier_google_highlight($text, $search)
```

```
    {
        $colors = array('#FFFF00','#00FFFF','#99FF99','#FF9999','#FF66FF',
                        '#880000','#00AA00','#886800','#004699','#990099');

        $terms = array();
        preg_match_all('/(".+?"|\S+)/', $search, $m);
        foreach (array_unique($m[0]) as $s) {
            $terms[] = str_replace('"', '', $s);
        }

        $r = $text;
        for ($i = 0; $i < count($terms); $i++) {
            $blocks = preg_split('/(<.+?'.'>)/s', $r, -1,
                            PREG_SPLIT_NO_EMPTY | PREG_SPLIT_DELIM_CAPTURE);
            $r = '';
            for ($j = 0; $j < count($blocks); $j++) {
                if (substr($blocks[$j], 0, 1) != '<') {
                    $replace = '<b style="color:'.($i / 5 % 2 ? 'white':'black').
                               ';background-color:'.$colors[$i % 10].'">\\1</b>';
                    $blocks[$j] = preg_replace('/('.preg_quote($terms[$i]).')/i',
                                        $replace, $blocks[$j]);
                }
                $r .= $blocks[$j];
            }
        }
        return $r;
    }
?>
```

Now that the plug-in file is in place, let's create a simple example to use it.

Create a new PHP script called example_google_highlight.php and put the following content into it:

```
<?php
include_once('libs/Smarty.class.php');
$smarty = new Smarty;

$results = array(
    'Management Team',
    'Customer Service',
    'Professional Services'
);
$search_keywords = 'professional service team';
$smarty->assign(array(
    'search_results' => $results,
    'keywords'       => $search_keywords
));

$smarty->display(example_google_highlight.tpl');
?>
```

Now create the accompanying template file, called example_google_highlight.tpl, which uses the google_highlight modifier:

```
<html>
<head>
<title>Example Corp.</title>
</head>
<body>

Search results:<br />
<ul>
{section name="i" loop=$search_results}
  <li>{$search_results[i]|google_highlight:$keywords}</li>
{sectionelse}
```

190

```
    <li>No results could be found for '{$keywords}'.</li>
{/section}
</ul>

Displaying results 1 - {$search_results|@count}.

</body>
</html>
```

Open that PHP script in your web browser, and you should see the following:

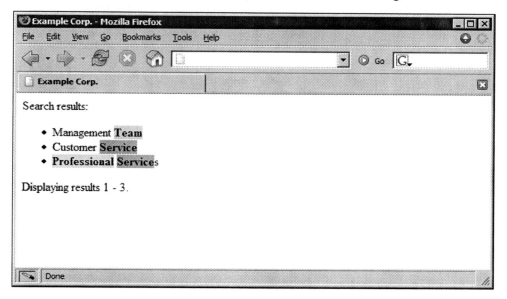

Obviously this is a pretty simple example, but you can probably see how this could be extremely useful when you need to help your users visually by displaying where the search keywords were found in a document title or body.

We could also implement something similar to automatically highlight search keywords when users are redirected by search engines with an output filter.

Writing your own Plug-ins

Before going off and writing your own plug-ins, please be aware of the naming convention that is used by Smarty to load plug-ins on demand. Basically, Smarty will parse your template, and as soon as it finds a particular function that it doesn't already support by default, it will load the associated plug-in file. So if you tried to use the `fsize_format` modifier plug-in described above, Smarty will try to load a file called `modifier.fsize_format.php` that should be located in Smarty's plug-in directory.

So the naming convention is the following:

```
type.function_name.php
```

function_name should be replaced with whatever the name of your plug-in is, and type by the type of your plug-in. The options for type are:

Type	String to use in plug-in filename
Functions	`function`
Modifiers	`modifier`
Block functions	`block`
Compiler functions	`compiler`
Resources	`resource`
Inserts	`insert`
Prefilters	`prefilter`
Postfilters	`postfilter`
Output filters	`outputfilter`

The last three options are covered in more detail in the next chapter, but we list them here for completeness' sake.

Inside each plug-in file you should create a function with the following naming convention:

```
smarty_type_function_name()
```

So to drive the point home: If you have a function plug-in called `auto_link_urls`, then the filename should be called `function.auto_link_urls.php` and the function name should be `smarty_function_auto_link_urls()`.

Plug-in Types

You can create several types of plug-ins, as listed above. Here are the main characteristics of each plug-in type.

Functions

Function plug-ins are the most common plug-ins available. They allow programmers to develop extra features that are executed when the function is called from within the templates. If any output is produced while the function is being executed, it will be placed where the function was within the template.

While the implementation for this type of plug-in varies widely with each type of need, some of these are outstanding plug-ins for your use. One of them is called *SmartyPaginate*, and was developed by the main author behind Smarty itself. It's a cross between a PHP class and a Smarty plug-in used to handle data set pagination within HTML pages. This is very useful for web developers and is available at `http://www.phpinsider.com/php/code/SmartyPaginate/`.

Modifiers

Modifier plug-ins take the value of the variable that they are being called against, and are allowed to change it. One common usage of plug-ins is to modify strings to highlight search keywords. Another very common usage is to treat values and escape embedded HTML or JavaScript input, to avoid XSS (Cross-Site Scripting) vulnerabilities.

Block Functions

This type of plug-in allows you to perform a set of changes to a given block of text. You could also use this type of plug-in to extend the built-in control structures of Smarty to allow for a new {while} function, for instance. We will take a detailed look at block functions in Chapter 12, where a block function is used to dynamically translate the content found within its tags.

Another pretty interesting example is the *RSSBlock* plug-in, available at http://smarty.incutio.com/?page=RSSBlock. This plug-in fetches an RSS feed and iterates over its items. For instance, the following is what is needed to fetch the last three news items from the PHP.net website:

```
{rss file="http://www.php.net/news.rss" length="3"}
  <a href="{$rss_item.link}" target=_blank> {$rss_item.title} </a><br>
{/rss}
```

Compiler Functions

Compiler functions are executed only when Smarty is in the process of compiling the templates into PHP scripts. This may be useful to programmatically add PHP code to the resulting compiled template, but that's also possible with output filters.

Prefilters, Postfilters, and Output Filters

Filters are covered in detail in Chapter 11.

Resources

Resource plug-ins allow you to change the way Smarty looks for templates. For instance, consider the following template source:

```
{include file="test.tpl"}
```

And this one:

```
{include file="file:test.tpl"}
```

The above templates do exactly the same thing: open the file test.tpl from the disk and include the output on the given template. However, you can customize how this works by assigning different resources for templates. You could create a special db resource that would make Smarty call a special plug-in to get the content of a given template, like:

```
{include file="db:test.tpl"}
```

However, this type of feature won't be needed for most web applications.

Inserts

Insert plug-ins are very similar to how the built-in {include} function works, but insert plug-ins are never cached, so that can be a way to overcome a platform limitation if you need to have refreshed data on a cached template.

This type of plug-in is very useful for certain cases in which you would like Smarty not to cache your template output, such as when you are generating advertising banners on the fly and changing the template output to include them. In that specific scenario, Smarty's caching feature, while extremely useful, will go against your business requirements and will need to be circumvented.

For instance, if you use the following code on your template:

```
{insert name="getRandomBanner" siteid="php" sectionid="articles"}
```

Smarty will in turn look for the insert_getRandomBanner function in your PHP script (which could come from included files and such), and pass the siteid and sectionid parameters as one associative array, as the first argument to this PHP function. This function is supposed to return the appropriate value to Smarty, which will replace the {insert} tag with it. So if you wanted to handle those requests, the following would be a good example of that function:

```php
<?php
function insert_getRandomBanner($params)
{
    if ($params['siteid'] == 'php') {
        $html = '<a href="/click.php?id=1"><img src="/banners/php.gif"></a>';
    } elseif ($params['siteid'] == 'asp') {
        $html = '<a href="/click.php?id=2"><img src="/banners/asp.gif"></a>';
    } else {
        $html = '<a href="/click.php?id=0"><img src="/banners/def.gif"></a>';
    }

    return $html;
}
?>
```

The function above returns different results based on the siteid parameter.

Registering Plug-ins

So while Smarty will dynamically load plug-ins that are not already loaded when they are used in templates, you can also register a plug-in manually via the following methods:

Type	Method Signature to Register a Plug-in
Functions	void register_function(string name, mixed impl [, bool cacheable [, mixed cache_attrs]])
Modifiers	void register_modifier(string name, mixed impl)
Block functions	void register_block(string name, mixed impl [, bool cacheable [, mixed cache_attrs]])
Compiler functions	void register_compiler_function(string name, mixed impl [, bool cacheable])
Resources	void register_resource(string name, array functions)
Inserts	No need for one—you pass the function name on the template file itself.

Please note that the parameter called `impl` in the table refers to the function or method name that Smarty will call, and it can be one of the following:

- A string variable holding the function name
- An array of the form `array($object, 'method_name')`
- An array of the form `array('class_name', 'method_name')`

Anyway, this feature to dynamically load plug-ins from PHP is good because you can quickly plug some custom code into your Smarty templates without having to create a separate plug-in file for it, or even following the function naming scheme on that file. As an example, we will quickly create a new function to print out the current version numbers of both PHP and Smarty.

- Let's create a new PHP script called `example_platform_info.php` to test our new plug-in:

```php
<?php
include_once('include/Smarty.class.php');
$smarty = new Smarty;
$smarty->config_dir = 'templates';

$smarty->register_function('platform_info', array('Info',
 'printPlatformDetails'));

class Info
{
    function printPlatformDetails($params, &$smarty)
    {
        echo 'Powered by PHP ' . phpversion();
        echo ' and Smarty ' . $smarty->_version;
    }
}

$smarty->display('templates/example_platform_info.tpl');
?>
```

As you can see, we registered a function called `platform_info`, and asked Smarty to statically call the method name `printPlatformDetails` within the `Info` class. There's no need to even set the function arguments on that method, but we need to have access to the `$smarty` variable to dynamically display the version number.

- Create a new template file called `example_platform_info.tpl` to print out the output of our plug-in:

```
<html>
<head>
<title>Example Corp.</title>
</head>
<body>

Welcome to our home page!

<hr>
{platform_info}

</body>
</html>
```

- And this is what it will output once you run that script on your own web server:

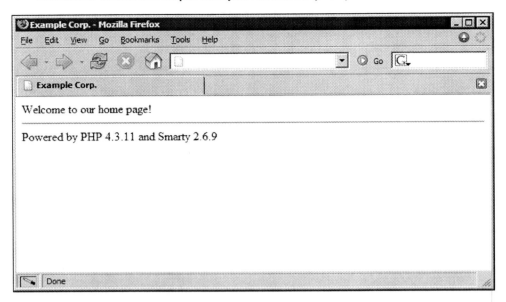

So that gives a simple idea of what's possible through custom plug-ins. Of course, there's a very big distinction between plug-in developers (usually programmers) and designers, but both of them need to work together to implement new features or widgets in templates. Some of the plug-in types described above will not be relevant to designers, such as a compiler function plug-in, but normal function plug-ins or even modifier plug-ins are highly relevant to their work. Have that in mind when you create your own template functions, so they are simple to use by someone who may not be a coder.

Next, let's create a few more complicated plug-ins.

Example Plug-in: Calendar

Our first example plug-in will be used to dynamically build a table containing the days of a particular month, just like what you would see if you opened your existing calendar application, like Microsoft Outlook, iCal, or Evolution. You should be able to specify what month and year you want from the template file, but if those parameters are not used, the current month and year will be used instead.

After running our calendar plug-in we expect the following output:

If possible the plug-in should be as simple to use as calling the function like:

```
{calendar month=4 year=2005}
```

As described before, if the month and year parameters are not provided, the current date will be used instead.

So to get that far, let's first create the PHP script and Smarty template that will be used to call our plug-in.

Create a new PHP script called example_calendar.php and put the following content in it:

```php
<?php
include_once('libs/Smarty.class.php');
$smarty = new Smarty;

$smarty->display('example_calendar.tpl');
?>
```

Follow this up by creating our template file, called example_calendar.tpl:

```
<html>
<head>
<title>Example Corp.</title>
</head>
<body>

<p><h2 style="text-align: center;">April 2005</h2></p>
{calendar month=4 year=2005}

</body>
</html>
```

Now that we have the requirements clearly specified, let's work on the plug-in itself. Since we know that this will need to be a function plug-in, and the name of the function is {calendar}, the resulting plug-in filename will be function.calendar.php and the PHP function inside it will have to be called smarty_function_calendar.

```php
<?php
/*
 * Smarty plugin
 * File:      function.calendar.php
 * Type:      function
 * Name:      calendar
 * Purpose:   Displays a calendar view of a month
 * Example:   {calendar}
 *            {calendar month=4 year=2005}
 * Install:   Drop into plug-in directory
 */
function smarty_function_calendar($params, &$smarty)
{
    extract($params);
    $html_result = '';

    $time = time();
    // if the 'month' parameter is not used, then
    // use the current month instead
    if (!isset($month)) {
        $month = date("n", $time);
    }
    // if the 'year' parameter is not used, then
    // use the current year instead
    if (!isset($year)) {
        $year = date("Y", $time);
    }
    // unix timestamp for the first day of this month
    $first_day_ts = mktime(0, 0, 0, $month, 1, $year);

    // create the table header
    $html_result = '<table border="1">';
    $html_result .= '<tr>
                        <th width="14%">Sunday</th>
                        <th width="14%">Monday</th>
                        <th width="14%">Tuesday</th>
                        <th width="14%">Wednesday</th>
                        <th width="14%">Thursday</th>
                        <th width="14%">Friday</th>
                        <th width="14%">Saturday</th>
                    </tr>';
```

This is simple. The code simply checks for the optional month and year parameters and uses the current day's month and year if they are not provided.

Next it will get a little more complicated, since we will have to dynamically display the first day of the month on whatever day of the week it ends up on. That is, April 1st 2005 may end up on a Friday, but the next month will not.

The code will also have to be sufficiently flexible to handle more than four weeks worth of days, since if the first day of the month starts on a Saturday, the month will have five weeks, and so on. Furthermore, the code will need to figure out how many days a specific month will have.

```php
$current_day = 1;
$current_week = 1;
// total days within this month
$total_days = date("t", $first_day_ts);
```

```
        // the week day number that the first day of the
        // month falls on (Sunday = 0; Saturday = 6)
        $first_day = date("w", $first_day_ts);

        // loops through the days
        while ($current_day <= $total_days) {
            $html_result .= '<tr>';
            for ($i = 0; $i < 7; $i++) {
                if ((($current_week == 1)
                        && ($i >= $first_day)) ||
                        (($current_week > 1)
                        && ($current_day <= $total_days))) {
                    $html_result .= '<td valign="top">';
                    $html_result .= $current_day ;
                    if ((isset($values)) && (!empty($values[$current_day]))) {
                        $html_result .= $values[$current_day];
                    } else {
                        $html_result .= ' ';
                    }
                    $html_result .= '</td>';
                    $current_day++;
                } else {
                    $html_result .= '<td> </td>';
                }
            }
            $html_result .= '</tr>';
            $current_week++;
        }
        $html_result .= '</table>';

        print $html_result;
    }
?>
```

Running the PHP script above will generate the wanted output. Here are some possible ideas to reuse this code and expand on it:

- A set of optional parameters that would allow you to specify a stylesheet class name to be used on the heading of the calendar table, and another one for the actual day cells. Maybe even a different class name for the currently selected day.

- A parameter to allow you to specify the content in each of those table cells, so you could display meetings or appointments that you have on them, project deadlines, holidays, birthdays that you want to keep track of, etc.

The calendar plug-in is a pretty neat idea as a function plug-in, since it allows you to separate logic related to the layout (i.e. creating this HTML table of days on a month) from your normal business logic code.

Example Plug-in: Auto-link URLs

Now let's create a modifier plug-in to dynamically create anchors out of URLs embedded within text that we want to display on web pages. That's a nice usability feature for your users, creating links automatically and saving your users from having to know HTML syntax or even having to do a few extra steps on a web application.

While previously we provided an actual plug-in file that contained the source code for the `calendar` function, this time we will reuse some existing PHP code, and turn it into a modifier plug-in. The trick here is that we will use regular expressions to automatically turn text sections such as `http://www.example.com` or even `www.example.com` into actual HTML anchors.

You could use this plug-in for a wide variety of tasks, such as displaying user-entered text that is not already in HTML format, or even displaying plain text documents such as emails, which often contain URLs like the above example ones.

The PHP code is pretty simple, but by no means is it complete in that it will handle any type of URL. Here's a new PHP script that we will include into another script, called `class.misc.php`, which will be stored in your `libs` directory:

```php
<?php
class Misc
{
    function autoLinkURLs($text)
    {
        $text = preg_replace("'(\w+)://([\w\+\-\@\=\?\.\%\/\:\&\;]+)(\.)?'",
"<a href=\"\\1://\\2\">\\1://\\2</a>", $text);
        $text = preg_replace("'(\s+)www\.([\w\+\-
\@\=\?\.\%\/\:\&\;]+)(\.\s|\s)'", "\\1<a
href=\"http://www.\\2\">www.\\2</a>\\3" , $text);
        return $text;
    }
}
?>
```

Since we are re-using this existing code, we will use the `register_modifier` routine to dynamically tell Smarty that it should use this method to modify the given template variable.

Create a new file called `example_auto_link_urls.php` and put the following content in it:

```php
<?php
include_once('libs/Smarty.class.php');
$smarty = new Smarty;

include_once('libs/class.misc.php');
$smarty->register_modifier('auto_link_urls', array('Misc',
'autoLinkURLs'));

$content = 'Welcome to our web site!

If you have any questions, please contact us by filling up the form at:
http://www.example.com/contact.php

The Management.';
$smarty->assign(array(
    'content' => $content
));

$smarty->display('example_auto_link_urls.tpl');
?>
```

Here's the source of the associated template file, called `example_auto_link_urls.tpl`:

```html
<html>
<head>
<title>Example Corp.</title>
</head>
```

```
<body>

{$content|nl2br|auto_link_urls}

</body>
</html>
```

And the output that this PHP script produces once it is requested:

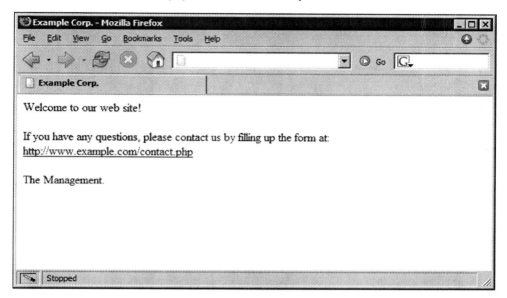

Summary

We went through the basic concepts of Smarty plug-ins, such as their overall architecture and design. The low-level details of writing your own plug-ins were also described, such as plug-in types, and naming conventions for plug-in filenames and function names.

Several of the plug-ins cited were found through the public Smarty website, and the third-party Smarty Wiki website, but you should also refer to search engines when trying to find new plug-ins. Not every developer remembers to go back to the central repositories to store a copy of their plug-ins.

Also, the three example plug-ins developed on this chapter are good stepping stones for more flexible and complex plug-ins, so feel free to use those on your own projects.

Remember that the act of creating a new plug-in is only restricted by your imagination, so always take enough time to think around good plug-in designs, especially with regard to plug-in types. Always remember to choose the appropriate plug-in type for whatever task you need to perform.

But most of all, remember the design objective of templates—separating business logic from layout logic. This means keeping your templates as simple as possible.

11
Filters

While the majority of Smarty plug-ins consists of functions and modifiers, another type of plug-in called filters gives you some extra functionality. Filters allow you to create plug-ins that interact deeply with the inner workings of Smarty, by setting PHP function callbacks that will be executed when certain phases of template parsing and execution are met.

Three different types of filters are:

- Prefilter
- Postfilter
- Output filter

Prefilters

Prefilter plug-ins are called right before the compilation of Smarty templates into PHP scripts. This is a perfect solution for certain tasks related to the template sources themselves, such as removing unwanted swear words. This is especially useful for content management systems where users are allowed to exchange content on Smarty templates. Another useful action is stripping comments and extra white space from JavaScript files, in order to optimize the download size of your utility files.

The **jStrip** plug-in does exactly that and is available at the Smarty Wiki: `http://smarty.incutio.com/?page=jStrip`.

Postfilters

Postfilter plug-ins are similar to prefilter ones, but they are executed after the compilation of Smarty templates into PHP scripts. This is useful in some cases to add some extra PHP code to the compiled template code, such as special headers or extra XML declarations.

Another example comes from the **rel2abs** plug-in, which replaces all relative URLs in a template file with the corresponding absolute URI version. It is available at `http://ownmedia.net/products/`.

Output Filters

Output filter plug-ins are called when Smarty is actually ready to display the output of the generated compiled template to the browser. This is different from the previous type because postfilter plug-ins are executed on the compiled templates before they are saved to disk.

Be extra careful with the details on this one, as output filters will not be executed until the output is generated when the template is executed. After the output is modified by this type of filter, it is only saved into Smarty's cache system (if that is indeed enabled).

Creating Filters

There are three main ways to create filters and make them available on Smarty templates:

- Register a filter plug-in at run time and point Smarty to a PHP function callback from within the template script by using one of the `register_*filter` functions.
- Tell Smarty to automatically load a filter from the plugin directory with the `load_filter` function.
- Manually set the `autoload_filters` Smarty property to make it load the appropriate filters automatically for you.

Let's go over these different ways now. To register a filter plug-in at run time, you need to use one of the following Smarty functions:

Type	Method signature to register a plug-in
Prefilters	`void register_prefilter(mixed impl)`
Postfilters	`void register_postfilter(mixed impl)`
Output filters	`void register_outputfilter(mixed impl)`

Please note that the parameter called `impl` above refers to the function or method name that Smarty will call, and it can be one of the following:

- A string value holding the function name
- An array of the form `array($object, 'method_name')`
- An array of the form `array('class_name', 'method_name')`

When actually writing the PHP code for the filter plug-ins, follow these rules for the function arguments:

Type	Function signature when writing the filter
Prefilters	`string function_name(string source, object smarty)`
Postfilters	`string function_name(string source, object smarty)`
Output filters	`string function_name(string output, object smarty)`

What this means is that for filter plug-ins, Smarty will pass the template source or template output as the first argument and the special Smarty object as the second argument to your PHP function, and expect you to return the modified source or output from that function.

Registering a Filter at Run Time

As an example, here's how you would use `register_outputfilter` to register an output filter at run time:

```php
<?php
include_once('libs/Smarty.class.php');
$smarty = new Smarty;

function highlight($output, &$smarty)
{
    // highlight the word "smarty" on our template source
    return str_replace('smarty', '<b>smarty</b>', $output);
}

$smarty->register_outputfilter('highlight');

$smarty->display('templates/example1.tpl');
?>
```

As you can see, the PHP function is being registered at run time with Smarty, and it will return a modified version of the output, highlighting the word *Smarty*. While this is a very simple example, we will expand it soon with a more complex version to dynamically highlight search keywords.

You could also pass an array to `register_outputfilter` (or any of the other `register_*filter` functions) to tell Smarty to call the given class or object method, as shown below:

```php
<?php
include_once('libs/Smarty.class.php');
$smarty = new Smarty;

class Misc
{
    function highlight($output, &$smarty)
    {
        // highlight the word "smarty" on our template source
        return str_replace('smarty', '<b>smarty</b>', $output);
    }
}

$smarty->register_outputfilter(array('Misc', 'highlight'));

$smarty->display('templates/example1.tpl');
?>
```

Manually Loading a Filter

There's also another way to load filters into Smarty, and that is the usual way of creating separate plug-in files, and storing them into a predefined directory. Smarty will then include the given filter plug-in file, and use it when needed.

Continuing with the standard format of the `register_*filter` functions, the filter plug-in filename should conform to these rules:

Type	String to use in plug-in filename
Prefilters	`prefilter`
Postfilters	`postfilter`
Output filters	`outputfilter`

For instance, if you would like to create an output filter plug-in called `append_benchmark_data`, then the filename should be `outputfilter.append_benchmark_data.php`. If the same plug-in were supposed to be a prefilter one, then the filename would be `prefilter.append_benchmark_data.php`, and so on. This filter plug-in file should be saved under Smarty's `plugin` sub-directory.

The same rules apply for the function name to be placed within the plug-in file. For our first example above of an output filter plug-in called `append_benchmark_data`, we would need to create the following PHP script:

```php
<?php
function smarty_outputfilter_append_benchmark_data($source, &$smarty)
{
    global $benchmark;

    $source .= '<div id="benchmark">';
    $source .= 'Generated in ' . $benchmark . ' secs.';
    $source .= '</div>';

    return $source;
}
?>
```

The plug-in above will append some extra HTML to the generated output from a template, and will return that modified output, referenced above in the `$source` variable.

Now that we have the plug-in file created correctly, we still need to tell Smarty that we want it to use this filter when processing templates. Since this is a manual process, you will use the `load_filter` Smarty method to do this, as shown next:

```php
<?php
include_once('libs/Smarty.class.php');
$smarty = new Smarty;

$smarty->load_filter('output', 'append_benchmark_data');

$smarty->display('templates/example1.tpl');
?>
```

The first parameter to the `load_filter` method is the filter type (possible values are *pre*, *post*, and *output*). This method will tell Smarty that we want it to use this plug-in.

Automatically Loading a Filter

One obvious downside of the previous method of loading a filter plug-in is that you need to use the `load_filter` method on every template that you want the filter to execute. What if you want the filter to run on your entire website or application? This can be done by automatically loading filters with the `autoload_filters` Smarty property.

We can do this by changing the value of this variable directly in the Smarty source code. Look for the `smarty.class.php` file and change the `autoload_filters` variable, as shown next:

```php
<?php
// inside Smarty.class.php ..

    /**
     * This indicates which filters are automatically loaded into Smarty.
     *
     * @var array array of filter names
     */
    var $autoload_filters = array('output' => array('append_benchmark_data'));

// ..
?>
```

The change above will tell Smarty to always load the given output filter plug-in. You will still need to create the plug-in file and name the function within it as explained in the previous section.

If you would always like to load several different types of filters, you can do so by specifying the appropriate filter type in the `autoload_filters` variable, as shown next:

```php
<?php
// inside Smarty.class.php ..

    /**
     * This indicates which filters are automatically loaded into Smarty.
     *
     * @var array array of filter names
     */
    var $autoload_filters = array(
                'output' => array('append_benchmark_data'),
                'pre'    => array('remove_comments', 'hide_emails'),
                'post'   => array('prepend_compilation_data')
        );

// ..
?>
```

As you can see, we are now registering one output filter, two prefilter plug-ins, and another postfilter one.

Filter #1: Remove HTML Comments

One of the classic examples for a pre-filter plugin is one that removes HTML comments from templates. Usually these comments are only relevant for you while developing your website or web application, so it makes sense to remove them to decrease the download size for your pages. This will not result in any visible changes to your templates or pages, but your users will appreciate the extra effort.

Create a new PHP script called `remove_comments.php` with the following content:

```php
<?php
include_once('libs/Smarty.class.php');
$smarty = new Smarty;

function remove_html_comments($source, &$smarty)
{
    // remove any html comments from the template source, even
    // if they span multiple lines
    return preg_replace('/<!--.*-->/Ums', '', $source);
}

$smarty->register_prefilter('remove_html_comments');
$smarty->display('remove_comments.tpl');
?>
```

Here is the source for the matching template file, called `remove_comments.tpl`:

```
<!--
This page will serve as...
-->

<html>
<head>
<title>Removing HTML Comments</title>
</head>

<body>

<!-- page title -->
<h1>Removing HTML Comments</h1>

<!-- real content starts here -->
<p>
   In order to remove HTML comments, you must
   create a Smarty filter.
</p>

</body>
</html>
```

Notice the HTML comments in bold above. Our objective here is to completely remove those entities to save some bandwidth. Now try running the `remove_comments.php` script with your web browser, and you should see the rendered page. View the source of that page, and it should look like the following:

```
<html>
<head>
<title>Removing HTML Comments</title>
</head>

<body>

<h1>Removing HTML Comments</h1>

<p>
   In order to remove HTML comments, you must
   create a Smarty filter.
</p>

</body>
</html>
```

Voilà! We now have the source without any HTML comments, but if you are paying extra attention, you should have noticed that where the HTML comments were, we now have empty lines. For extra neatness, let's go ahead and improve our PHP script just a little bit to trim off any extra whites pace lines like the ones in the above file.

We are lucky that Smarty already provides an output filter plug-in exactly for this purpose, called `trimwhitespace`. Since it is already included in the Smarty distribution, all we need to do is to load that filter. Here's the modified source code for `remove_comments.php`:

```php
<?php
include_once('libs/Smarty.class.php');
$smarty = new Smarty;

function remove_html_comments($source, &$smarty)
{
    // remove any html comments from the template source, even
    // if they span multiple lines
    return preg_replace('/<!--.*-->/Ums', '', $source);
}

$smarty->register_prefilter('remove_html_comments');
$smarty->load_filter('output', 'trimwhitespace');
$smarty->display('remove_comments.tpl');
?>
```

No changes are needed to our existing `remove_comments.tpl` template. Try running the modified PHP script with your web browser, and you should see a different HTML source for that page, as shown next:

```
<html>
<head>
<title>Removing HTML Comments</title>
</head>
<body>
<h1>Removing HTML Comments</h1>
<p>
In order to remove HTML comments, you must
create a Smarty filter.
</p>
</body>
</html>
```

No visual changes will happen with these modifications, but the overall page size should decrease a little bit. While the improvements are not impressive with this example template, the changes to larger pages will be significant.

Filter #2: Benchmark Information

One common need for web developers is to profile their PHP applications to make sure that everything is properly set up performance-wise. The usual way to go about this is to record the time in various portions of code, and then calculate how long each section is taking, and then take measures to improve the performance.

However, when doing this benchmarking work manually by timing each section of the PHP code, the template parsing and compilation steps will not be taken into account. One of the workarounds is to create a postfilter plug-in that simply records the time when Smarty finishes the compilation of a template, and another output filter plug-in to calculate the processed time and add the generated benchmark information to the template output. We will go over these plug-ins next, starting with the overall benchmark script.

The following is the full source code for benchmark.php, which is based on the previous example's source code:

```php
<?php
ini_set("include_path",".;c:\\server\\xampp\\php\\pear\\");
include_once('libs/Smarty.class.php');
$smarty = new Smarty;
$smarty->force_compile = TRUE;

// PEAR's Benchmark::Timer package
include_once('Benchmark/Timer.php');
$bench = new Benchmark_Timer;
$bench->start();

function register_compilation($source, &$smarty)
{
    $GLOBALS['bench']->setMarker('Finished compilation');
    return $source;
}

function append_benchmark_results($output, &$smarty)
{
    $GLOBALS['bench']->stop();
    $results = $GLOBALS['bench']->getProfiling();
    $output .= '<table border=1>';
    $output .=
'<tr><th>Marker</th><th>Diff</th><th>Total</th></tr>';
    for ($i = 0; $i < count($results); $i++) {
        $output .= '<tr><td>' . $results[$i]['name'] . '</td>';
        $output .= '<td>' . $results[$i]['diff'] . '</td>';
        $output .= '<td>' . $results[$i]['total'] .
'</td></tr>';
    }
    $output .= '</table>';

    return $output;
}

function remove_html_comments($source, &$smarty)
{
    // remove any html comments from the template source, even
    // if they span multiple lines
    return preg_replace('/<!--.*-->/Ums', '', $source);
}

$bench->setMarker('Before display');

$smarty->register_prefilter('remove_html_comments');
$smarty->register_postfilter('register_compilation');
$smarty->register_outputfilter('append_benchmark_results');
$smarty->load_filter('output', 'trimwhitespace');
$smarty->display('benchmark.tpl');
?>
```

There are many details here. To start with, we are using PEAR's `Benchmark_Timer` class to measure the time difference between each portion of the code. You will need to replace the path on the second line of your code with the path where your PEAR installation is stored. We also created two new filter plug-ins, one being a postfilter called `register_compilation` to be run right after the compilation phase of Smarty. The other one called `append_benchmark_results` will be executed right before sending the template output back to the web browser, and we will use it to calculate the profile information, and build a HTML table with the results.

One very important detail here is critical to making these plug-ins work the way we want them to, and that is to force Smarty to always compile the given template. We do that by setting Smarty's `force_compile` property to TRUE. If that change is not done, the postfilter plug-in will only be executed when a template is compiled into a PHP script. Since the benchmarking example is strictly for development purposes, we are performing this change. You should be sure to disable this property when pushing your website or application onto its production server, as forcing the compilation of templates will result in a big performance loss.

Here is the source for the `benchmark.tpl` template file, which is the same as the previous example's template:

```
<!--
This page will serve as...
-->

<html>
<head>
<title>Removing HTML Comments</title>
</head>

<body>

<!-- page title -->
<h1>Removing HTML Comments</h1>

<!-- real content starts here -->
<p>
  In order to remove HTML comments, you must
  create a Smarty filter.
</p>

</body>
</html>
```

Now try running the given PHP script with your web browser. You should see something similar to the following figure:

The benchmark results are properly appended to the template output, and you can analyze them to decide potential changes to your PHP code. The first column displays the label of each benchmark marker, while the other columns display the difference in time between that marker and the previous one, and the total execution time so far. As you can see, the total execution time is 0.047573 seconds for this trial run.

Filter #3: Compress Output with gzip

Another very good use case for output filters is to change the way your website or application sends data back to the web browser. One of the best ways to improve the performance of your pages is to compress them, either with the Remove HTML Comments filter plug-in discussed before, or with a real compression algorithm, such as gzip. Most web browsers nowadays work very well with compressed web pages.

We will now reuse an output filter that will compress the template output from Smarty, and return that compressed output to the web browser, while passing the appropriate HTTP headers. The filter plug-in source code is available below. Copy this source code and save it as a file named outputfilter.gzip.php under Smarty's plugin sub-directory.

```php
<?php
/*
 * Type:      outputfilter
 * Name:      gzip
 * Author:    Joscha Feth, joscha@feth.com
 */
function smarty_outputfilter_gzip($tpl_source, &$smarty)
```

```
{
        /* the compression level to use
           default: 9
           ------------------------------------
                     0 -> 9
           less compressed -> better compressed
           less CPU usage  -> more CPU usage
           ------------------------------------
        */
        $compression_level = 9;

        /* force compression, even if gzip is not sent in HTTP_ACCEPT_ENCODING,
           for example Norton Internet Security filters this, but 95% percent of
           the browsers do support output compression, including Firefox
           and Opera.
           default: yes
        */
        $force_compression = true;

        // message to append to the template source, if it is compressed
        $append_message = "\n<!-- zlib compression level " .
              $compression_level . " -->";

        // only compress the output if:
        // - headers were not sent yet
        // - zlib extension is available
        // - caching is disabled in smarty
        // - correct encoding is sent, or compression is forced
        if ((!headers_sent()) && (extension_loaded('zlib')) && (!$smarty->caching)
              && (strstr($_SERVER['HTTP_ACCEPT_ENCODING'], 'gzip')
              || $force_compression)) {
           $tpl_source = $tpl_source . $append_message;
           $tpl_source = gzencode($tpl_source, $compression_level);
           header('Content-Encoding: gzip');
           header('Vary: Accept-Encoding');
           header('Content-Length: ' . strlen($tpl_source));
        }
        return $tpl_source;
}
?>
```

The only requirement for this output filter to work, as is true with other filter plug-ins, is for you to load it in PHP scripts with the `load_filter()` method, or add it to the list of automatically loaded filters with the `autoload_filters` property. No visual changes should be noticed, but the output will be compressed and therefore the load times for most pages will be quicker.

Filter #4: Search Engine Highlight

One of my favorite plug-ins from Chapter 10 was used to dynamically highlight search keywords entered by users of your site. Let's expand on that idea and do the same thing for users reaching our website from a search engine, such as Google. The HTTP protocol mandates that web browsers pass a special value each time users click on links from one page to another, so the resulting page is aware of where this user came from. This is called the referrer field, and it may be empty if the user types the URL of your web page manually on the address bar of the browser.

This is very useful information for websites, as it allows you to see how effective a marketing campaign is going, or even a source of information to generate reports based on where people often find out about your website.

So, using that special bit of information, let's build a Smarty output filter plug-in that will be called each time the parsed and generated template is about to be sent to the browsers of our users, and then highlight any search keywords that may have been used.

Let's create a new set of PHP script and template files to show how this can be done.

Create a new PHP script called `search_highlight.php` and put the following on it:

```php
<?php
include_once('libs/Smarty.class.php');
$smarty = new Smarty;

$smarty->load_filter('output', 'search_highlight');
$smarty->display('search_highlight.tpl');
?>
```

Create a new template file called `search_highlight.tpl` with the following:

```html
<html>
<head>
<title>Highlighting Search Keywords</title>
</head>
<body>

<h1>Random Content</h1>

<p>Lorem ipsum dolor sit amet, consectetuer adipiscing elit. Pellentesque
leo. Aliquam vulputate enim eget enim. Quisque nunc. Pellentesque habitant
morbi tristique senectus et netus et malesuada fames ac turpis egestas.
Donec iaculis. Duis dignissim pede vitae purus. Ut gravida eros sit amet
sapien. Donec ipsum leo, porta in, rhoncus vitae, eleifend vel, mi.
aecenas non risus.</p>

</body>
</html>
```

As you can see above, this is a simple template file, but we can use it as a test page for our search highlight plug-in. This is because we want to stress that an output filter doesn't really require any template-level changes, since the changes that it will perform will be done after the template is parsed and generated.

Create a new plug-in file called `outputfilter.search_highlight.php` and put the following content in it:

```php
<?php
/*
 * Smarty plugin
 *
 * File:      outputfilter.search_highlight.php
 * Type:      output filter
 * Name:      search_highlight
 * Purpose:   Automatically highlights search keywords when a user is redirected
 *            by Google to your web pages.
 * Install:   Drop into plugin directory, then use load_filter() to manually
 *            load plugin into Smarty, or setting the $autoload_filters
 *            variable.
 */
require_once $smarty->_get_plugin_filepath('modifier', 'google_highlight');

function smarty_outputfilter_search_highlight($tpl_output, &$smarty)
```

```
{
    // check if we have anything on HTTP_REFERER
    $referrer = getenv('HTTP_REFERER');
    if (!empty($referrer)) {
        $pieces = parse_url($referrer);
        // only highlight search keywords if the user
        // is coming from google.com
        if (stristr($pieces['host'], 'google.com')) {
            $params = explode('&', $pieces['query']);
            $query = array();
            foreach ($params as $param) {
                list($key, $value) = explode('=', $param);
                $query[$key] = urldecode($value);
            }
            // only do something if we have actual
            // search keywords to play with
            if (!empty($query['q'])) {
                $tpl_output = smarty_modifier_google_highlight($tpl_output,
                                                               $query['q']);
            }
        }
    }
    return $tpl_output;
}
?>
```

What this code is really doing is going through the HTTP_REFERER environment variable, which will be populated by the full URL of the search engine page that was generated by our user searching for something. For instance, if I were to search on the words random and sapien on Google, the URL would end up being the following:

```
http://www.google.com/search?hl=en&q=random+sapien&btnG=Google+Search
```

> You can manually change the $referrer variable on the search highlight plug-in to the URL given above if you don't want to wait for Google to crawl your website.

The code will first check if there's anything in the HTTP_REFERER variable, then check if the referrer page was a search page from Google, then parse the query string on that URL for the actual search keywords, which are stored in $query['q']. After parsing the URL and finding the search keywords, we can re-use the existing Google Highlight plug-in to highlight the search terms.

The following is what you should see if you run the PHP script on your browser. However, you would need to have searched Google for the words random and sapien for the page to change as it did below.

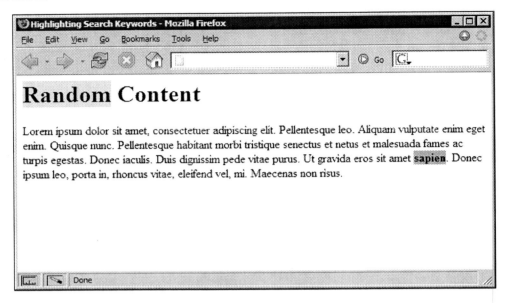

Summary

We covered all the low-level details about filter plug-ins, including how to create them from scratch by writing your own separate plug-in files, and how to point Smarty to existing PHP functions, classes, or objects to perform changes to templates. We also discussed the differences between the three types of filter plug-ins, and which type is appropriate for a particular function.

Keep in mind the low-level details of how Smarty compiles templates into PHP scripts, and how that affects the inner workings of postfilter plug-ins. Remember to set force_compile to TRUE when implementing things in your development environment, but also remember to disable it when pushing your website or application to a production environment.

Filters are a perfect way to tweak things in Smarty to provide a better service to your users, so always keep that in mind when thinking about a new feature.

12
Internationalization

One of the holy grails of web development is internationalization (usually shortened to i18n), especially as the industry matures and needs to cover several different markets and countries. Often you would like to have the same website translated into different languages, and that's the subject of this chapter.

So while this is a pretty simple objective, we do face some challenges on how to properly design the architecture of your web application while using Smarty. We have two different types of requirements for this:

- Translation of an entire set of templates into different languages, while keeping the templates the same. This is a perfect example for a web application, since you want to deliver the same features to all of your users.

- Translation of a complete set of templates, and changing a few of the templates for some of the different languages. That usually happens for websites that require some changes to a few pages, like special promotions that are only supposed to happen on a specific country, and so on.

We will go over the first requirement over the next few sections. You should be able to extend it pretty easily to be able to override any of the default translated templates with a customized one later on.

Translation Infrastructure: Gettext

The gold standard for the i18n community, as far as UNIX (and consequently PHP) is concerned, is the use of the Gettext project. This is a set of GNU tools designed to help translate text strings on the fly, from one language to another.

Gettext works by extracting text strings from source code files, and storing them into message catalogs. These catalog files are stored into a directory structure that is standardized, and the translated string is looked up at run time. If the translated text string is not found, or doesn't have a translation available yet, the original one will be used instead.

So here's an overview of the workflow:

- Extract the text strings from source code into a message catalog file, named `messages.po` by default.

- Edit the `messages.po` file to translate the text strings into another language.

- When done, convert the modified `messages.po` into a binary file, called `messages.mo` by default, that the Gettext extension will understand and use.

- Set up the PHP code to use the appropriate translation file, by using the Gettext functions.

We will go over the details of using Gettext with PHP over the next few sections.

Configuring PHP with Gettext

In order to make any of the following examples work with your PHP installation, you will need to make sure that you have the Gettext extension enabled. Follow the following instructions:

- Open your `php.ini` configuration file, usually located in `c:\windows\php.ini` on Windows systems.

- Scroll down in this file until you find a bunch of lines that begin with the expression `;extension=`. All the lines that contain a semi-colon on the front are disabling the given PHP extensions.

- Find the line that contains the `php_gettext.dll` extension, and remove the semi-colon from the beginning of the line. If there is no line in there, write a new line, like so:

  `extension=php_gettext.dll`

- Save the changes in the `php.ini` file.

- Restart the web server software that you are using.

These instructions are for Windows users. If you are using Linux or another UNIX operating system then these steps will not work for you. The easiest way to do this is to get the appropriate package from your vendor, such as an RPM, Debian package, or even installing from FreeBSD's port collection.

Simple PHP Example

Let's go through the workflow outlined before about how to work with Gettext, and translate a simple PHP script, to get a handle on how everything works together. You need to create a new PHP script called `simple_example.php` and put the following content in there:

```php
<?php
$language_code = 'pt_BR';
putenv("LANG=$language_code");
setlocale(LC_ALL, $language_code);

$domain = 'smartybook';
bindtextdomain($domain, './locale');
textdomain($domain);
?>
```

```
<h1>Translation to Language Code: <?php echo $language_code; ?></h1>

<?php
echo gettext("A message to translate") . "<br />\n";
echo gettext("second message") . "<br />\n";
echo gettext("third message") . "<br />\n";
?>
```

There are several interesting things happening in the script above:

- We are creating a $language_code variable and setting the 'pt_BR' value in there. That's the language code for Brazilian Portuguese, which will be the target translation language for our script.

- After that, we set the LANG environment variable and the LC_ALL locale constant to that language code.

- Then, we create a $domain variable specifying the message domain. This is usually the name of your application, or website.

- The bindtextdomain function associates the domain with a given path. This tells Gettext where to look for the translated catalog files, which in our example will be smartybook.mo.

- The call to the textdomain function sets the default domain. This is used to tell Gettext which domain (similar to a word dictionary) to search for translated strings when calling the gettext function.

- Finally, the calls to the gettext function will return the actual translated text strings.

Of course, the PHP script given above will only work when we set up the proper Gettext files, and place them in the appropriate directories. We will take a look at setting up Gettext files in the next section. One important note here is that xgettext will only extract text strings contained within double quotes, and will completely ignore the ones found inside single quotes. So as a guideline for your PHP scripts, if you want to translate messages with Gettext, always use double quotes.

Setting Up the Gettext Files

Gettext works by looking through a local directory structure for the translated catalog files. Here's an example directory structure for an application that is translated to German and Brazilian Portuguese:

```
/locale
    /de
        /LC_MESSAGES
            smartybook.po
            smartybook.mo
    /pt_BR
        /LC_MESSAGES
            smartybook.po
            smartybook.mo
```

You can put the locale directory anywhere you want, since that's configurable on the call to the bindtextdomain function. The smartybook.po file is not necessary in those directories, but it's nice to keep everything together like that, to make things easier later when you need to update the translation files for a particular language.

As mentioned before, the first step in the whole translation process is to generate the message file, which in our example is called `smartybook.po`. There is a ready-to-use utility that will extract all text strings from a set of files, and that utility is called `xgettext`. Here's how to do this:

```
$ xgettext -o smartybook.po -n *.php
```

The command above will parse all PHP scripts on the current directory for text strings, and will output the ones it finds to the `smartybook.po` file. The -n switch is used to include extra information such as the filename and line number at which each text string was found.

By running that command, we end up with the following content on `smartybook.po`:

```
# SOME DESCRIPTIVE TITLE.
# Copyright (C) YEAR THE PACKAGE'S COPYRIGHT HOLDER
# This file is distributed under the same license as the PACKAGE package.
# FIRST AUTHOR <EMAIL@ADDRESS>, YEAR.
#
#, fuzzy
msgid ""
msgstr ""
"Project-Id-Version: PACKAGE VERSION\n"
"POT-Creation-Date: 2005-10-09 18:38-0400\n"
"PO-Revision-Date: YEAR-MO-DA HO:MI+ZONE\n"
"Last-Translator: FULL NAME <EMAIL@ADDRESS>\n"
"Language-Team: LANGUAGE <LL@li.org>\n"
"MIME-Version: 1.0\n"
"Content-Type: text/plain; charset=CHARSET\n"
"Content-Transfer-Encoding: 8bit\n"

#: simple_example.php:9
msgid "A message to translate"
msgstr ""

#: simple_example.php:10
msgid "second message"
msgstr ""

#: simple_example.php:11
msgid "third message"
msgstr ""
```

As you can see, `xgettext` found the three text strings that were passed to the `gettext` function and placed inside the message file. The file above will be used now to translate the three text strings into the proper translation in Brazilian Portuguese. The following snippet is the proper translated message file:

```
# Smarty Book
# Copyright (C) 2005 Joao Prado Maia
# This file is distributed under the same license as the PACKAGE package.
# Joao Prado Maia <jpm@pessoal.org>, 2005.
#
#, fuzzy
msgid ""
msgstr ""
"Project-Id-Version: Smarty Book\n"
"POT-Creation-Date: 2005-10-09 18:38-0400\n"
"PO-Revision-Date: 2005-10-09 18:38-0400\n"
"Last-Translator: Joao Prado Maia <jpm@pessoal.org>\n"
"Language-Team: Brazilian Portuguese Team <pt_BR@pessoal.org>\n"
"MIME-Version: 1.0\n"
"Content-Type: text/plain; charset=ISO-8859-1\n"
"Content-Transfer-Encoding: 8bit\n"
```

```
#: simple_example.php:9
msgid "A message to translate"
msgstr "Uma mensagem para traduzir"

#: simple_example.php:10
msgid "second message"
msgstr "segunda mensagem"

#: simple_example.php:11
msgid "third message"
msgstr "terceira mensagem"
```

Now that we finally have a translated message file, let's generate the binary message catalog. There's yet another utility to perform this task called msgfmt, and here's the usage:

```
$ msgfmt -o smartybook.mo smartybook.po
```

Now you should have a smartybook.mo catalog file to use. The last remaining step is to go back to the directory structure of the locale path, and move the files into the proper location. In our example, that would mean moving the smartybook.mo file into the locale/pt_BR/LC_MESSAGES directory:

```
$ mv smartybook.mo locale/pt_BR/LC_MESSAGES/
```

Now we should be ready to test it. Load the simple_example.php script with your web browser, and you should see the following output:

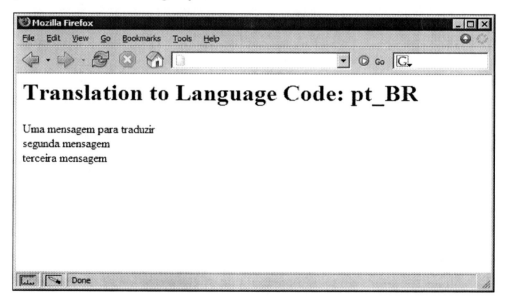

There you go! We now have a fully translated web page. Even though this is a simple example, you could expand its usage easily by parsing several PHP scripts and using the translated output in your application.

Using Gettext with Smarty

So while the previous example is interesting and gives us a nice introduction to how Gettext really works, and how to apply it to PHP scripts, our real objective is to use it with Smarty templates in some way that allows us to avoid having to duplicate the template structure across languages.

There are several ways to do this, which include the following:

- Create a special Smarty block function (called {translate}, perhaps), and translate the contents into a different language dynamically that way.

- Have each content section passed from PHP, and translated on the fly with the method that was described before.

- Pass the translated content to each template by using Smarty config files.

Each of those methods has its own weaknesses:

- By creating a block function, we lose the automatic extraction of text strings that comes from the use of the xgettext utility. Since it will not generate the PO files automatically for us, we will need to create a separate script to do that.

- By passing each content section from the PHP script, we will make the template files harder to use and maintain, since it will not be immediately clear which section we are changing at any time.

- Using Smarty config files brings the same problem, but with the extra complexity of having to use a different file for the translated text strings.

With that in mind, let's use a Smarty block function to translate the text strings, and worry about the automatic generation later, as it shouldn't be extremely difficult to parse the Smarty templates ourselves and create the PO file.

Hopefully, there's a ready-to-use Smarty plug-in designed exactly for this purpose. As people say on the Internet, if you need to do something, you are probably not the first one and an open-source project already exists. In this case the project is called *Smarty Gettext* and is being maintained by Sagi Bashari. It is licensed under both the GPL and LGPL licenses, so you are pretty much free to use it, make changes to it, and distribute those changes. You may want to check back on the project website at the following URL: http://sourceforge.net/projects/smarty-gettext/.

This project already includes everything we need, such as the block function (called {t} in this case), and also a separate PHP script that extracts text strings from Smarty templates into C files that will then be parsed by xgettext to generate the needed PO file.

In order to install this Smarty plug-in, all we need to do is to copy the source code file called block.t.php to the Smarty plug-ins directory.

Let's go over an example of translating text strings directly from Smarty templates. Since we already have a ready-to-use smartybook.mo catalog file, let's reuse the same text strings in our template. First, let's create a new PHP script called gettext1.php with the following content:

```php
<?php
include_once('libs/Smarty.class.php');
$smarty = new Smarty;
```

```
$language_code = 'pt_BR';
putenv("LANG=$language_code");
setlocale(LC_ALL, $language_code);

$domain = 'smartybook';
bindtextdomain($domain, './locale');
textdomain($domain);

$smarty->display('gettext1.tpl');
?>
```

This PHP script doesn't do anything fancy that we haven't seen before. It simply creates a Smarty object, and then sets up the required gettext environment with the functions we covered before. Here's the source for the gettext1.tpl template file:

```
<html>
<head>
<title>First Smarty-Gettext Example</title>
</head>
<body>
<h1>First Smarty-Gettext Example</h1>
<h2>#1: {t}A message to translate{/t}</h2>
<h2>#2: {t}second message{/t}</h2>
<h2>#3: {t}third message{/t}</h2>
</body>
</html>
```

As you can see, we are re-using the same text strings we used before, but this time we are using the {t} block function around them. That template code will pass the given text strings to the Smarty Gettext block plug-in, which will call the gettext function on them, and return the translated messages.

This is how the template looks like once executed:

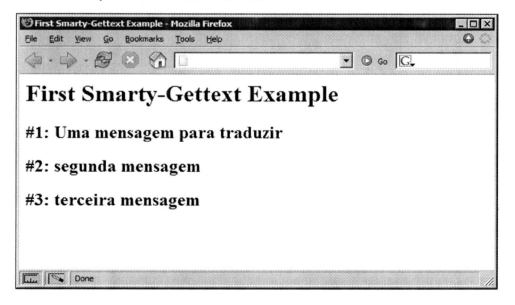

And that's exactly what we wanted it to look like. Now let's see what happens when you add a new text string to be translated, but there is no associated translation available on the `smartybook.mo` file. Change the `gettext1.tpl` template, and put the following content in it:

```
<html>
<head>
<title>First Smarty-Gettext Example</title>
</head>

<body>

<h1>First Smarty-Gettext Example</h1>

<h2>#1: {t}A message to translate{/t}</h2>
<h2>#2: {t}second message{/t}</h2>
<h2>#3: {t}third message{/t}</h2>
<h2>NEW: {t}fourth message{/t}</h2>

</body>
</html>
```

No changes are necessary on the PHP script itself. Reload the PHP script on your web browser, and you should see the following in there:

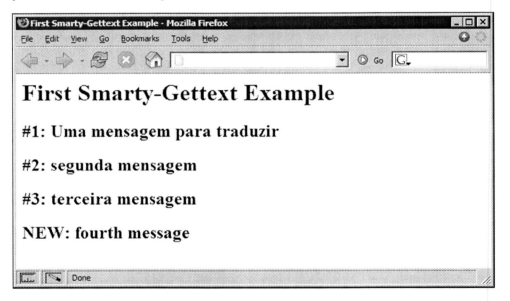

As you can see, the new text string was not translated, and the original message was returned by the plug-in. It might not be always simple to quickly spot a missing translation, but it's a nice feature to have in any case.

However, since our real objective is to have a completely translated website or application, let's go over the details of how to manage text strings on Smarty templates. It turns out that the Smarty Gettext plug-in already provides all the tools we need.

Generating a PO File

The first step to expand our usage of the Smarty Gettext plug-in is to start using the {t} block function on the other messages on our template file. Let's change it so that all the messages are translated on the fly.

The following is the source code for a new version of the gettext1.tpl template file, renamed to gettext2.tpl:

```
<html>
<head>
<title>{t}First Smarty-Gettext Example{/t}</title>
</head>

<body>

<h1>{t}First Smarty-Gettext Example{/t}</h1>

<h2>#1: {t}A message to translate{/t}</h2>
<h2>#2: {t}second message{/t}</h2>
<h2>#3: {t}third message{/t}</h2>
<h2>#4: {t}fourth message{/t}</h2>

</body>
</html>
```

We also need a new PHP script to accompany this template file. We will call this script gettext2.php and the following is its source code:

```
<?php
include_once('libs/Smarty.class.php');
$smarty = new Smarty;

$language_code = 'pt_BR';
putenv("LANG=$language_code");
setlocale(LC_ALL, $language_code);

$domain = 'smartybook';
bindtextdomain($domain, './locale');
textdomain($domain);

$smarty->display('gettext2.tpl');
?>
```

The Smarty Gettext plug-in comes with a PHP script called tsmarty2c.php, and it will extract all text strings between {t} and {/t}, and output the appropriate C code, which should then be used by xgettext to generate the PO file. Here's a walkthrough of how this works:

- First run the tsmarty2c.php utility to extract the text strings from the template. Here's the command that should be run:

  $ php -q tsmarty2c.php templates/gettext2.tpl > text_strings.c

- The text_strings.c file should contain the appropriate C code to be passed on to xgettext. Here's the source code of that file from the command above:

```
/* templates/gettext2.tpl */
gettext("First Smarty-Gettext Example");

/* templates/gettext2.tpl */
gettext("First Smarty-Gettext Example");
```

```
/* templates/gettext2.tpl */
gettext("A message to translate");

/* templates/gettext2.tpl */
gettext("second message");

/* templates/gettext2.tpl */
gettext("third message");

/* templates/gettext2.tpl */
gettext("fourth message");
```

- Now use the xgettext utility just as described previously in this chapter, but targeting this new C file. The following is the command that should be executed:

```
$ xgettext -o smartybook.po --join-existing --omit-header --no-location
text_strings.c
```

- And the following are the contents of the modified smartybook.po file:

```
# Smarty Book
# Copyright (C) 2005 Joao Prado Maia
# This file is distributed under the same license as the PACKAGE package.
# Joao Prado Maia <jpm@pessoal.org>, 2005.
#
#, fuzzy
msgid ""
msgstr ""
"Project-Id-Version: Smarty Book\n"
"POT-Creation-Date: 2005-10-09 18:38-0400\n"
"PO-Revision-Date: 2005-10-09 18:38-0400\n"
"Last-Translator: Joao Prado Maia <jpm@pessoal.org>\n"
"Language-Team: Brazilian Portuguese Team <pt_BR@pessoal.org>\n"
"MIME-Version: 1.0\n"
"Content-Type: text/plain; charset=ISO-8859-1\n"
"Content-Transfer-Encoding: 8bit\n"

msgid "A message to translate"
msgstr "Uma mensagem para traduzir"

msgid "second message"
msgstr "segunda mensagem"

msgid "third message"
msgstr "terceira mensagem"

msgid "First Smarty-Gettext Example"
msgstr ""

msgid "fourth message"
msgstr ""
```

- It worked perfectly! Now all we need to do is modify the PO file and translate the two new text messages. Here are the new translations:

```
msgid "First Smarty-Gettext Example"
msgstr "Primeiro Exemplo do Smarty-Gettext"

msgid "fourth message"
msgstr "quarta mensagem"
```

- After saving the changes, convert the modified file with the msgfmt utility, and move it into the appropriate location:

```
$ msgfmt -o smartybook.mo smartybook.po

$ mv smartybook.mo locale/pt_BR/LC_MESSAGES/
```

226

There you go. You should be able to open the `gettext2.php` PHP script with your web browser, and see the following output:

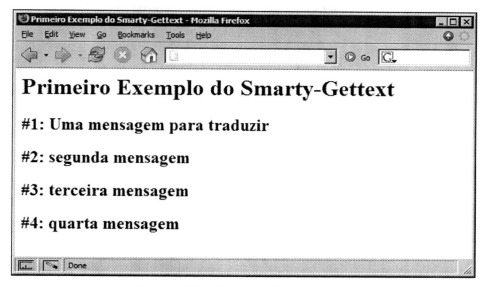

The output shows that our script is working fine, and all text messages are being translated on the fly. Let's look at some other more advanced features of this plug-in.

Advanced Features of Smarty Gettext

While the previous example was perfect for a simple web page, things start getting more complicated when we need to pass information from PHP to Smarty. This is what happens if we need to translate the following expression: There are X customers waiting for Y orders, where X and Y are both variable values.

For the expression above, we could just translate that expression by separately translating the following three messages:

- There are
- customers waiting for
- orders

We would then have to join them together afterwards. That's a valid way of doing this, but it's much more complex than having to translate just one phrase. It's also a potential translation problem as translators might not know what the context is for each of these expressions and even more because the required order of these expressions or the positions for the numbers might differ in different languages.

In any case, Smarty Gettext provides a nice and easy-to-use feature for these issues. You may pass parameters to a translated string, and the plug-in will take care of substituting the parameters in the resulting translated message. Let's go for a simple example of this feature.

Here's the source code for `parameters.php`:

```php
<?php
include_once('libs/Smarty.class.php');
$smarty = new Smarty;

$language_code = 'pt_BR';
putenv("LANG=$language_code");
setlocale(LC_ALL, $language_code);

$domain = 'smartybook';
bindtextdomain($domain, './locale');
textdomain($domain);

$smarty->assign('customers', 6);
$smarty->assign('orders', 9);

$smarty->display('parameters.tpl');
?>
```

The following are the contents of the associated template file, called `parameters.tpl`:

```html
<html>
<head>
<title>{t}Passing Parameters to Translations{/t}</title>
</head>

<body>

<h1>{t}Passing Parameters to Translations{/t}</h1>

<p>
{t 1=$customers 2=$orders}There are %1 customers waiting for %2 orders.{/t}
</p>

</body>
</html>
```

As you can see, we are passing two parameters to the text message. They are numeric arguments to make it easy for the actual translators. The plug-in feature will substitute the string %1 with the value of the template variable $customers, and it will replace %2 with the value of $orders.

By running the bundled `tsmarty2c.php` script against the `parameters.tpl` file, we will get the following source:

```c
/* templates/parameters.tpl */
gettext("Passing Parameters to Translations");

/* templates/parameters.tpl */
gettext("Passing Parameters to Translations");

/* templates/parameters.tpl */
gettext("There are %1 customers waiting for %2 orders.");
```

Now we just need to go through the usual process of generating the PO file from the C file, and then converting into the binary catalog file and moving it to the correct place. Here's the output when everything is done:

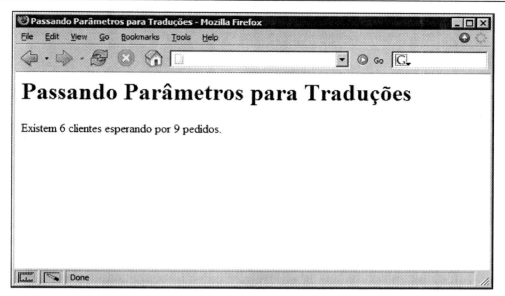

The Smarty Gettext plug-in is translating the message beforehand, and then replacing the parameters with the given template variables.

Summary

In this chapter, we went over the details of how to build a website or application that supports multiple languages, while at the same time being able to reuse the same Smarty templates for that. We learned a lot about what Gettext is, the history behind this important tool, and how to use that set of utilities with PHP and Smarty to accomplish our goals.

The main Gettext workflow of extracting text strings from PHP scripts or Smarty templates was used throughout this chapter, and the Smarty Gettext plug-in was introduced to help make this a possibility. The bundled scripts allow developers to plug Smarty templates into the normal Gettext workflow, and continue using the existing framework for translating templates and web pages.

We also covered the advanced features of the Smarty Gettext plug-in, such as numeric parameters. Dealing with that type of feature requires some tweaks to the way the translation usually works, but it should be simple to follow. This feature will definitely be needed as the complexity of your templates increases.

This chapter will help you build a strong foundation to grow from. Deploying multi-language websites and applications has never been easier!

Index

default, 87
escape, 87
indent, 88
lower, 89
nl2br, 89
regex_replace, 90
replace, 91
spacify, 91
string_format, 91
strip, 92
strip_tags, 93
truncate, 93
upper, 89
wordwrap, 94
modifiers, design concepts, 36
modifiers, types of plug-ins, 193
msgfmt command, Gettext, 221
must revalidate, cache-control header, 180

N

nested arrays, processing, 112
newsletter, real-world templates, 70
nl2br modifier, 89
no cache, cache-control header, 180
no store, cache-control header, 180
non-associative array, template design, 54

O

object-oriented programming (OOP), 36
optimization, design concepts, 35
optimizing Smarty applications, 176
output filter plug-ins, 204

P

page elements, reusing, 99
parameters, Smarty Gettext, 227
passing variables, 102
PEAR Benchmark_Timer class, 211
photo gallery template, advanced template
  development, 80
PHP code within templates, 73
PHP profiling, 177
PHP script translation, Gettext, 218
php.ini,
  Gettext configuration, 218
  Smarty Linux configuration, 16
  Smarty Windows configuration, 16

php_handling variable, 141
plug-ins, design concepts, 36
plug-ins, Smarty
  about, 13
  examples, 196
  File Size Format plug-in, 187
  filters, creating, 204
  finding and installing, 185
  Google Highlight plug-in, 189
  HTML List plug-in, 186
  output filter plug-ins, 204
  post-filter plug-ins, 203
  pre-filter plug-ins, 203
  registering, 194
  Smarty Gettext, 222
  types, 192
  writing plug-ins, 191
plug-ins, types of
  block functions, 193
  compiler functions, 193
  function, 192
  inserts, 194
  modifiers, 193
  resources, 193
plugins_dir variable, 139
postfilters,
  advanced template development, 77
  plug-ins, 203
  Smarty, 14
pre-filters
  plug-ins, 203
  advanced template development, 77
  Smarty, 14
presentation layer separation, 34
presentation logic layer, software design, 10
problem-solving perspective, 22
profiling PHP, 177
programmer, website building roles, 24
programmers, collaborating with, 46
programming, design concepts, 36
project manager, website building roles, 24
proxy revalidate, cache-control header, 180
public, cache-control header, 180

R

radio buttons, creating, 120
rdelim function, 110
real-world templates, 61
regex_replace modifier, 90

Thank you for buying Smarty: PHP Template Programming and Applications

Packt Open Source Project Royalties

When we sell a book written on an Open Source project, we pay a royalty directly to that project. Therefore by purchasing *Smarty: PHP Template Programming and Applications*, Packt will have given some of the money received to the Smarty project.

In the long term, we see ourselves and you—customers and readers of our books—as part of the Open Source ecosystem, providing sustainable revenue for the projects we publish on. Our aim at Packt is to establish publishing royalties as an essential part of the service and support a business model that sustains Open Source.

If you're working with an Open Source project that you would like us to publish on, and subsequently pay royalties to, please get in touch with us.

Writing for Packt

We welcome all inquiries from people who are interested in authoring. Book proposals should be sent to authors@packtpub.com. If your book idea is still at an early stage and you would like to discuss it first before writing a formal book proposal, contact us; one of our commissioning editors will get in touch with you.

We're not just looking for published authors; if you have strong technical skills but no writing experience, our experienced editors can help you develop a writing career, or simply get some additional reward for your expertise.

About Packt Publishing

Packt, pronounced 'packed', published its first book "*Mastering phpMyAdmin for Effective MySQL Management*" in April 2004 and subsequently continued to specialize in publishing highly focused books on specific technologies and solutions.

Our books and publications share the experiences of your fellow IT professionals in adapting and customizing today's systems, applications, and frameworks. Our solution-based books give you the knowledge and power to customize the software and technologies you're using to get the job done. Packt books are more specific and less general than the IT books you have seen in the past. Our unique business model allows us to bring you more focused information, giving you more of what you need to know, and less of what you don't.

Packt is a modern, yet unique publishing company, which focuses on producing quality, cutting-edge books for communities of developers, administrators, and newbies alike. For more information, please visit our website: www.PacktPub.com.

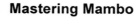

Mastering Mambo

ISBN: 1904811515   Paperback: 270 pages

A professional-level guide to Mambo's most powerful and useful features

1. Build e-commerce stores and discussion forums into Mambo

2. Make your site multilingual, accessible, and optimized for speed and search engines

3. Master DOCMAN, the document manager for Mambo, to turn your Mambo site into a dynamic repository of shared documents and files

4. Create custom layouts, modules, Mambots, and more

Building Websites with Joomla!

ISBN: 1904811949   Paperback: 250 pages

A step-by-step tutorial to getting your Joomla! CMS website up fast

1. Walk through each step in a friendly and accessible way

2. Customize and extend your Joomla! site

3. Get your Joomla! website up fast

For More Information: www.PacktPub.com

DATE DUE

JAN 1 3 2009		
NOV 3 0 2012		
DEC 0 3 2014		

Brodart Co.   Cat. # 55 137 001   Printed in USA

Printed in the United States
71461LV00004B/73